GRAPHIC SCIENCE

THE *WHIRLWIND* WORLD OF
HURRICANES

WITH
MAX AXIOM
SUPER SCIENTIST™

4D An Augmented Reading Science Experience

by Katherine Krohn | illustrated by Cynthia Martin and Al Milgrom

Consultant:
Matt Smith
Senior Research Scientist
University of Alabama in Huntsville

CAPSTONE PRESS
a capstone imprint

T0051039

Graphic Library is published by Capstone Press,
1710 Roe Crest Drive, North Mankato, Minnesota 56003.
www.capstonepub.com

Library of Congress Cataloging-in-Publication Data is available on the Library of Congress website.

ISBN: 978-1-5435-7250-6 (library binding)
ISBN: 978-1-5435-7547-7 (paperback)
ISBN: 978-1-5435-7254-4 (eBook PDF)

Summary: In graphic novel format, follows the adventures of Max Axiom
as he explains the science behind hurricanes.

Designer	*Media Researcher*	*Editor*
Alison Thiele	Wanda Winch	Mari Bolte
Colorist	*Production Specialist*	
Krista Ward	Laura Manthe	

Photo Credits
Capstone Studio: Karon Dubke, 29, back cover

All internet sites appearing in back matter were available and accurate
when this book was sent to press.

This is a Capstone 4D book!

Want fun videos that go with this book?

Just visit www.capstone4d.com

Use this password

hurricane.72506

Printed in the United States   5946

TABLE OF CONTENTS

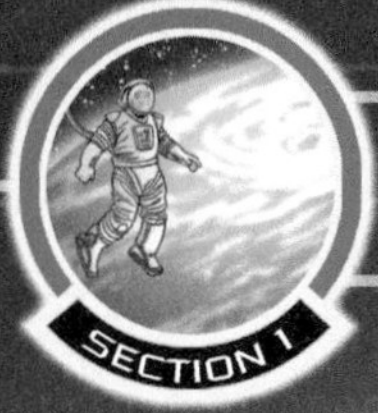
SECTION 1

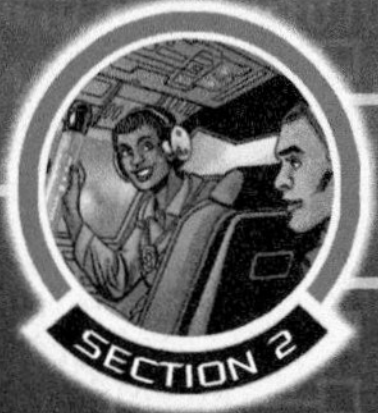
SECTION 2

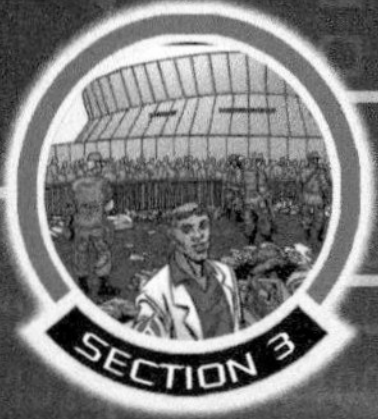
SECTION 3

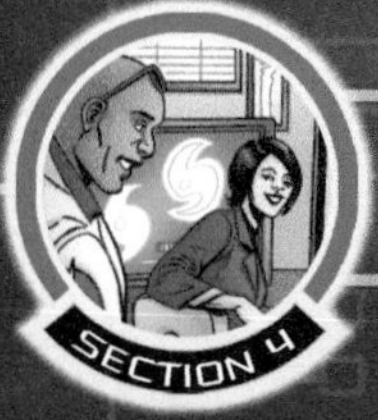
SECTION 4

SECTION 1 VIOLENT STORM

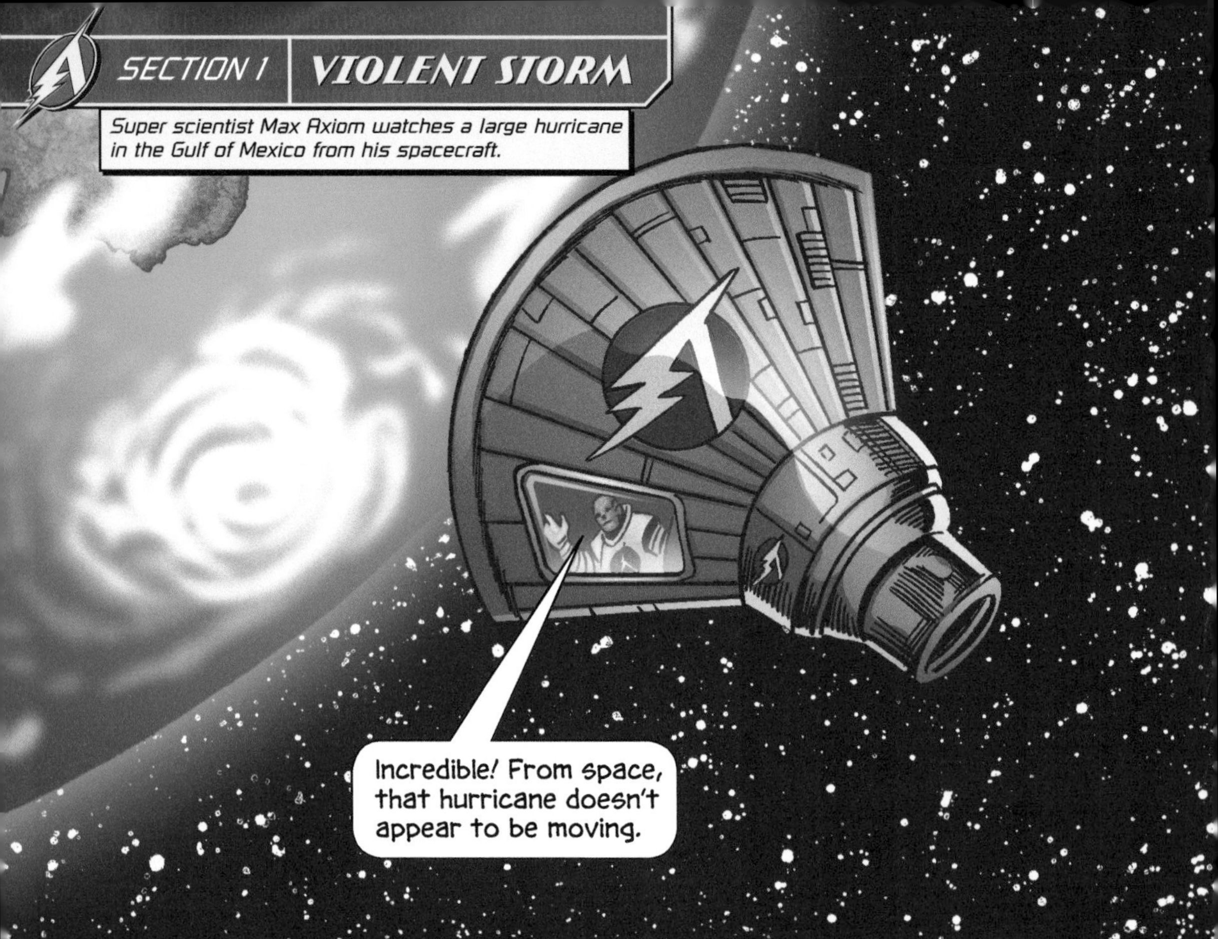
Super scientist Max Axiom watches a large hurricane in the Gulf of Mexico from his spacecraft.
Incredible! From space, that hurricane doesn't appear to be moving.

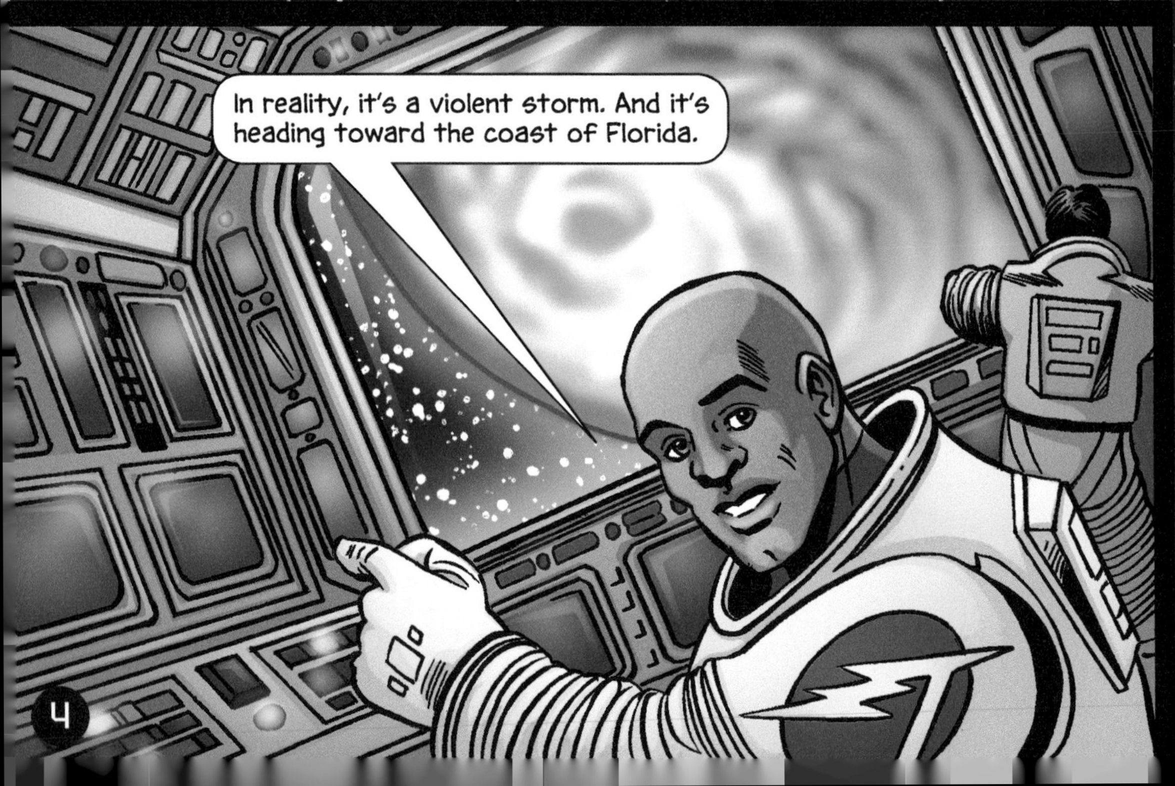
In reality, it's a violent storm. And it's heading toward the coast of Florida.

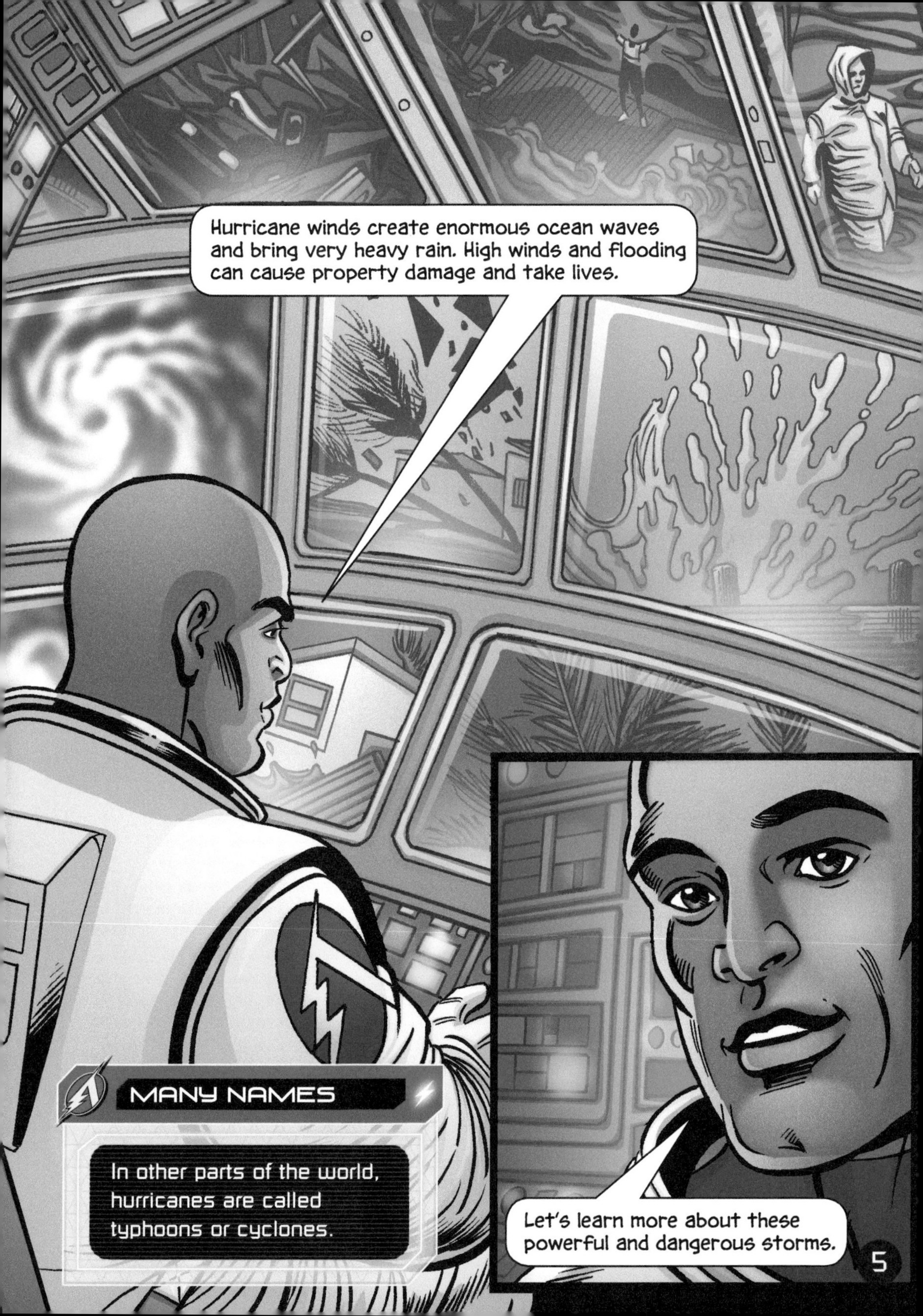
Hurricane winds create enormous ocean waves and bring very heavy rain. High winds and flooding can cause property damage and take lives.
MANY NAMES
In other parts of the world, hurricanes are called typhoons or cyclones.
Let's learn more about these powerful and dangerous storms.

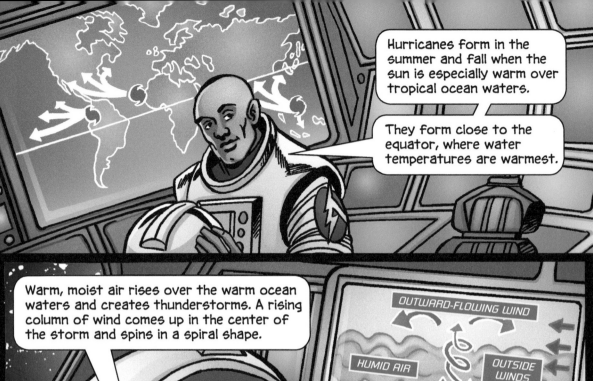

Hurricanes form in the summer and fall when the sun is especially warm over tropical ocean waters.

They form close to the equator, where water temperatures are warmest.

Warm, moist air rises over the warm ocean waters and creates thunderstorms. A rising column of wind comes up in the center of the storm and spins in a spiral shape.

OUTWARD-FLOWING WIND

HUMID AIR

OUTSIDE WINDS

RISING WIND

WARM OCEAN WATERS

The storm gains power and speed as it spins. As the storm spins faster, it grows more powerful. Let's take a closer look!

SPEEDY STORMS

ACCESS GRANTED: MAX AXIOM

A storm goes through a series of changes before becoming a hurricane. During the first stage, called a tropical depression, winds begin to rotate. Wind speeds reach 23 to 38 miles (37 to 61 kilometers) per hour. Then it turns into a tropical storm. During this stage, the storm becomes more organized and starts to resemble a hurricane. Wind speeds reach 39 to 73 mph (63 to 117 kph). When winds reach speeds of 74 mph (119 kph), the storm is finally called a hurricane.

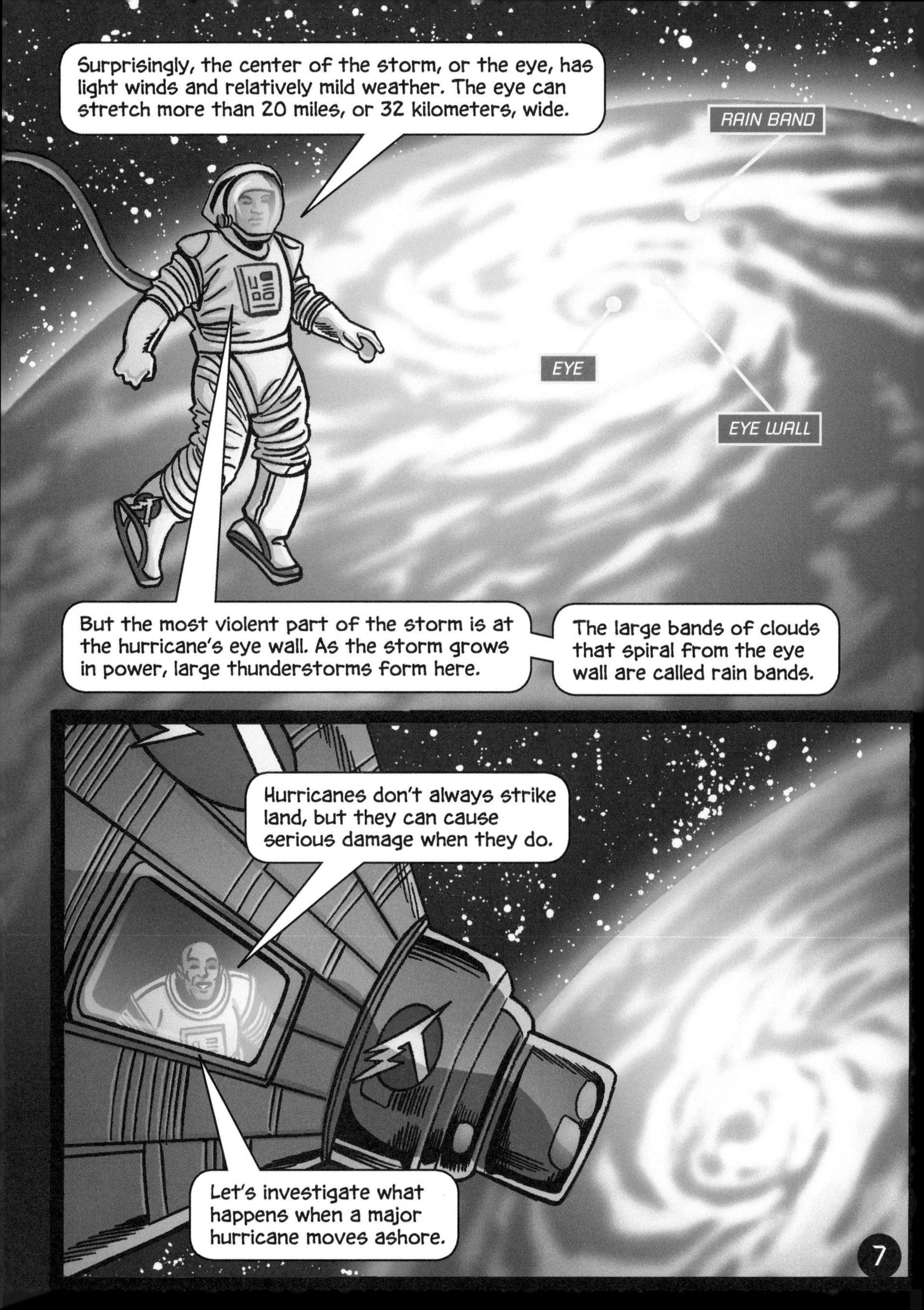
Surprisingly, the center of the storm, or the eye, has light winds and relatively mild weather. The eye can stretch more than 20 miles, or 32 kilometers, wide.
RAIN BAND
EYE
EYE WALL
But the most violent part of the storm is at the hurricane's eye wall. As the storm grows in power, large thunderstorms form here.
The large bands of clouds that spiral from the eye wall are called rain bands.
Hurricanes don't always strike land, but they can cause serious damage when they do.
Let's investigate what happens when a major hurricane moves ashore.

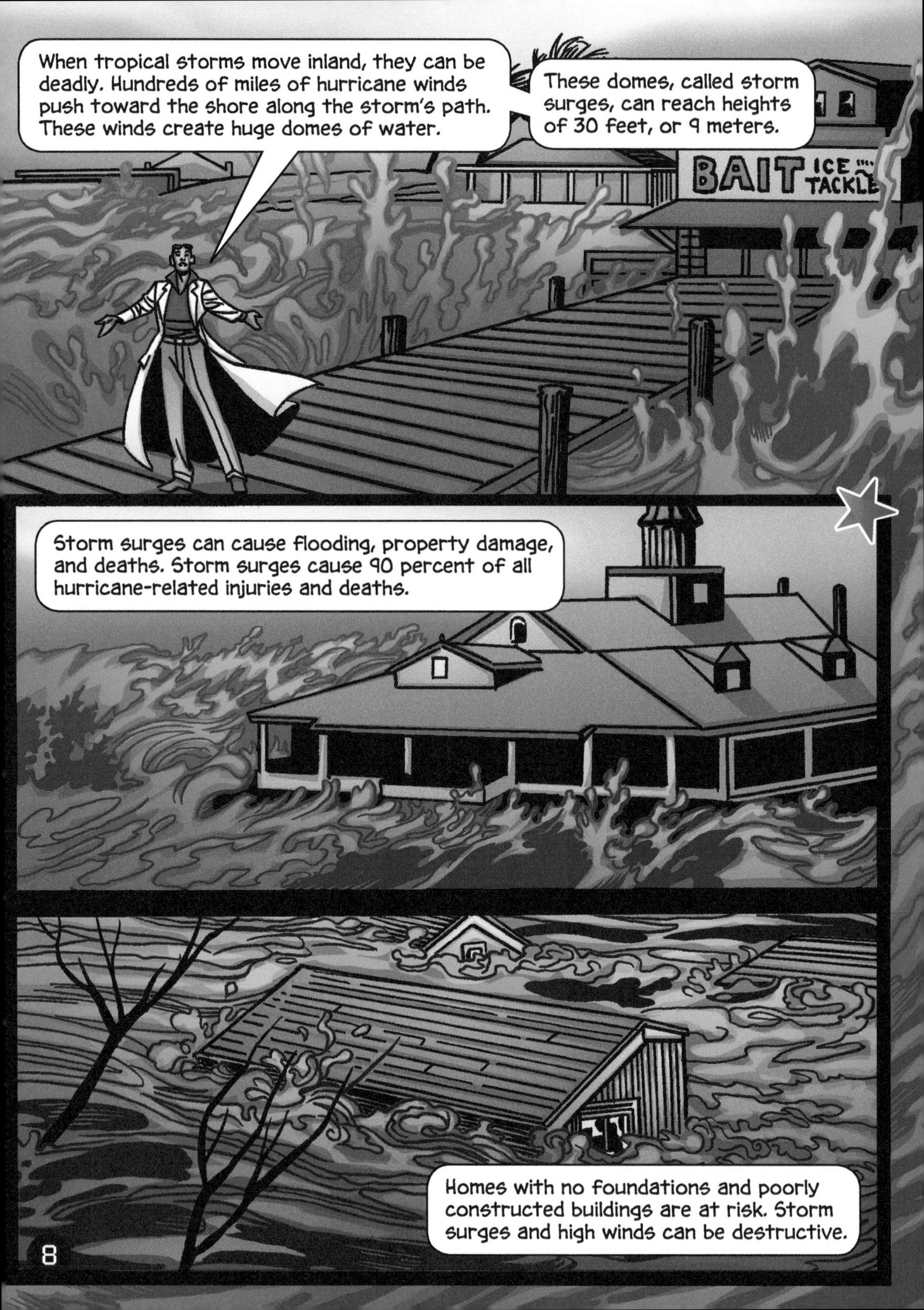
When tropical storms move inland, they can be deadly. Hundreds of miles of hurricane winds push toward the shore along the storm's path. These winds create huge domes of water.
These domes, called storm surges, can reach heights of 30 feet, or 9 meters.
BAIT ICE TACKLE
Storm surges can cause flooding, property damage, and deaths. Storm surges cause 90 percent of all hurricane-related injuries and deaths.
Homes with no foundations and poorly constructed buildings are at risk. Storm surges and high winds can be destructive.

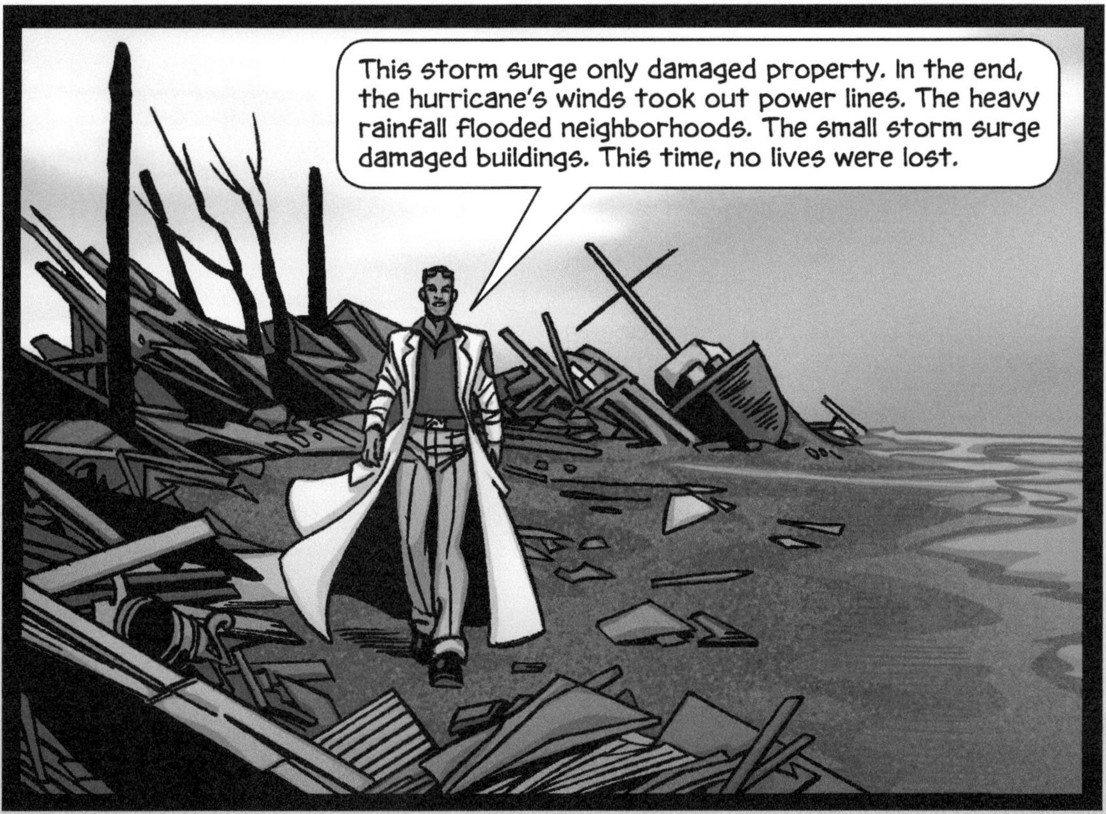
This storm surge only damaged property. In the end, the hurricane's winds took out power lines. The heavy rainfall flooded neighborhoods. The small storm surge damaged buildings. This time, no lives were lost.

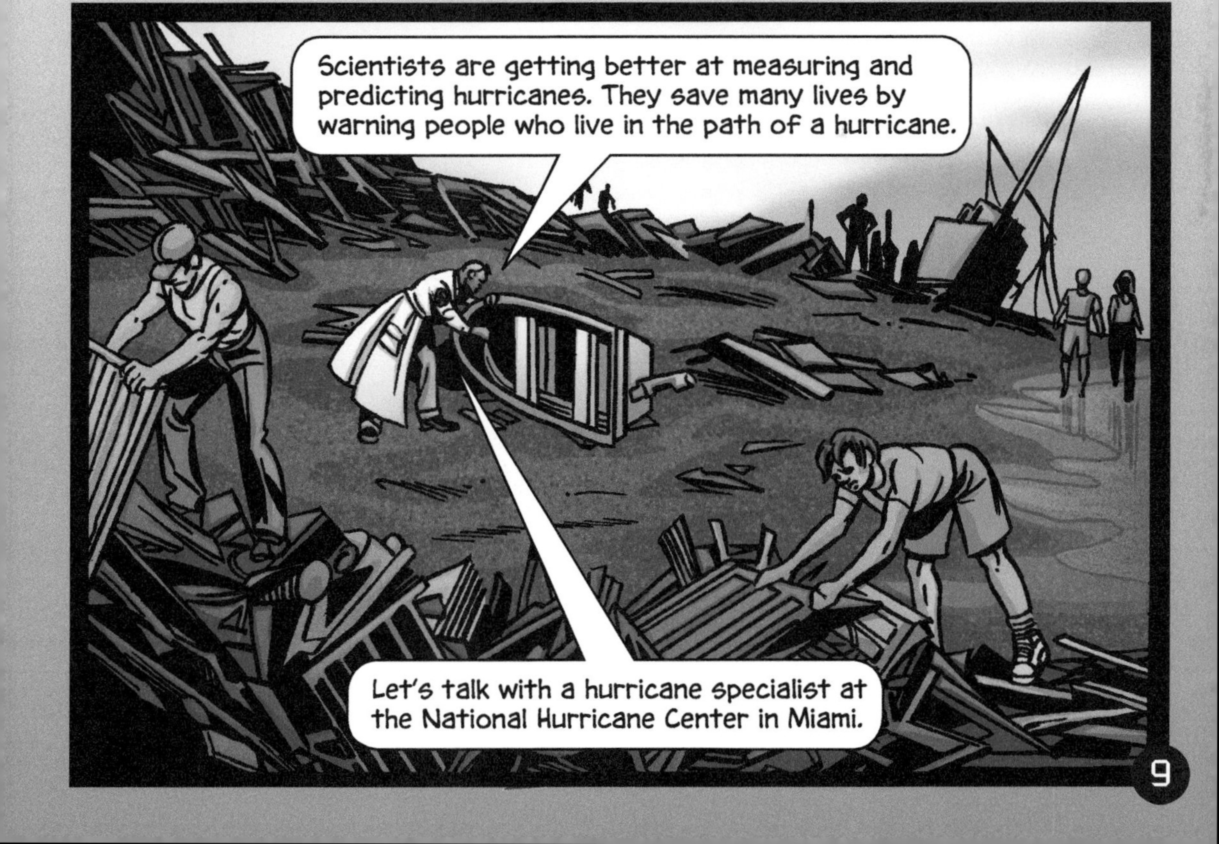
Scientists are getting better at measuring and predicting hurricanes. They save many lives by warning people who live in the path of a hurricane.
Let's talk with a hurricane specialist at the National Hurricane Center in Miami.

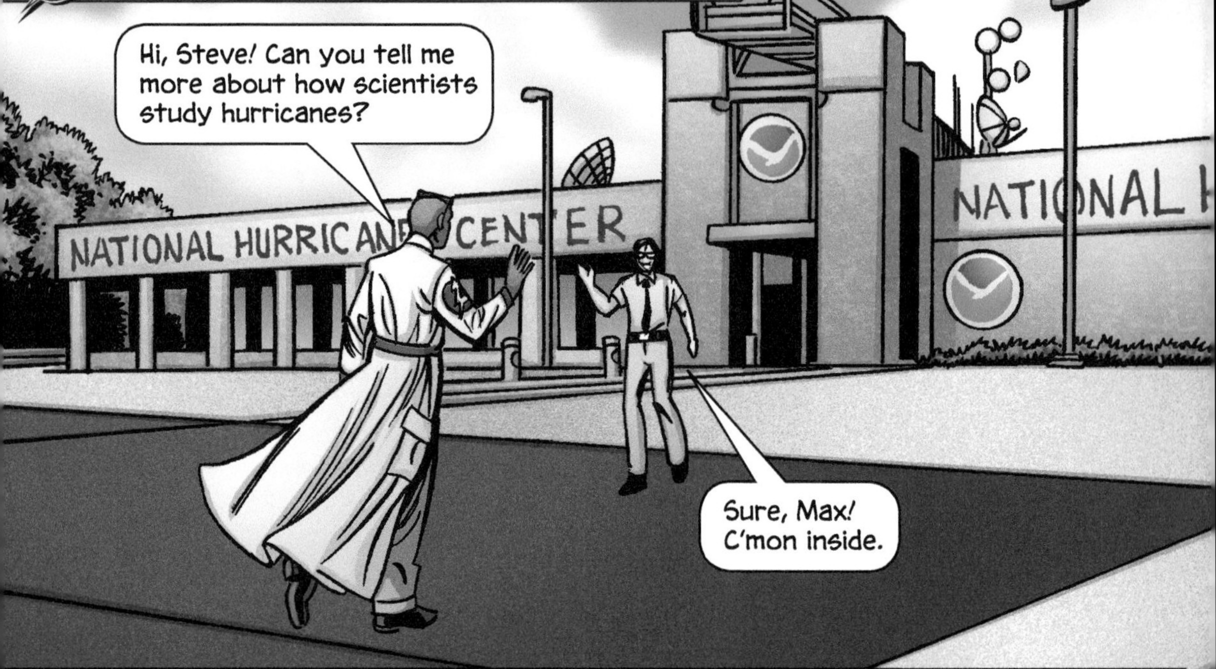
Hi, Steve! Can you tell me more about how scientists study hurricanes?
Sure, Max! C'mon inside.

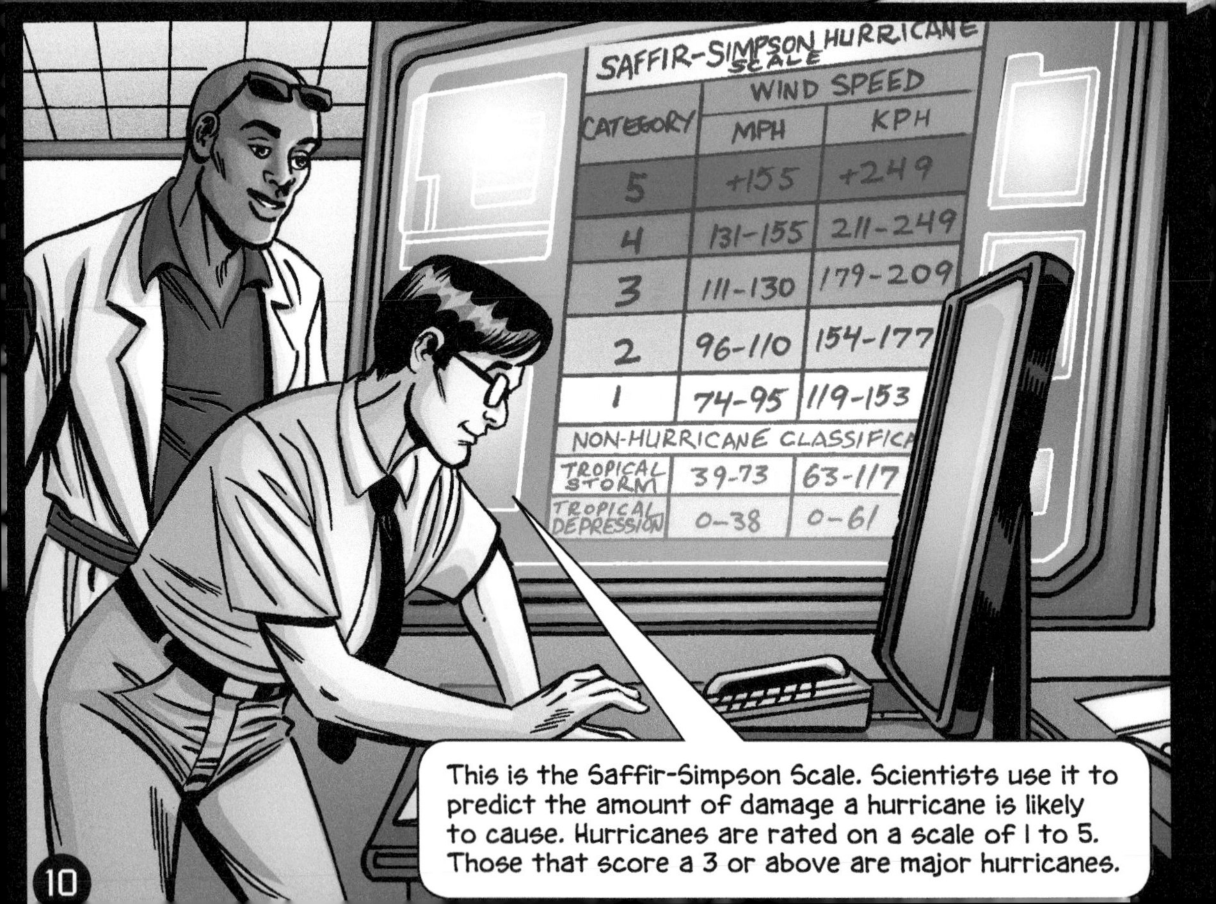
SAFFIR-SIMPSON HURRICANE SCALE
WIND SPEED
CATEGORY MPH KPH
5 +155 +249
4 131-155 211-249
3 111-130 179-209
2 96-110 154-177
1 74-95 119-153
TROPICAL STORM 39-73 63-117
TROPICAL DEPRESSION 0-38 0-61
This is the Saffir-Simpson Scale. Scientists use it to predict the amount of damage a hurricane is likely to cause. Hurricanes are rated on a scale of 1 to 5. Those that score a 3 or above are major hurricanes.

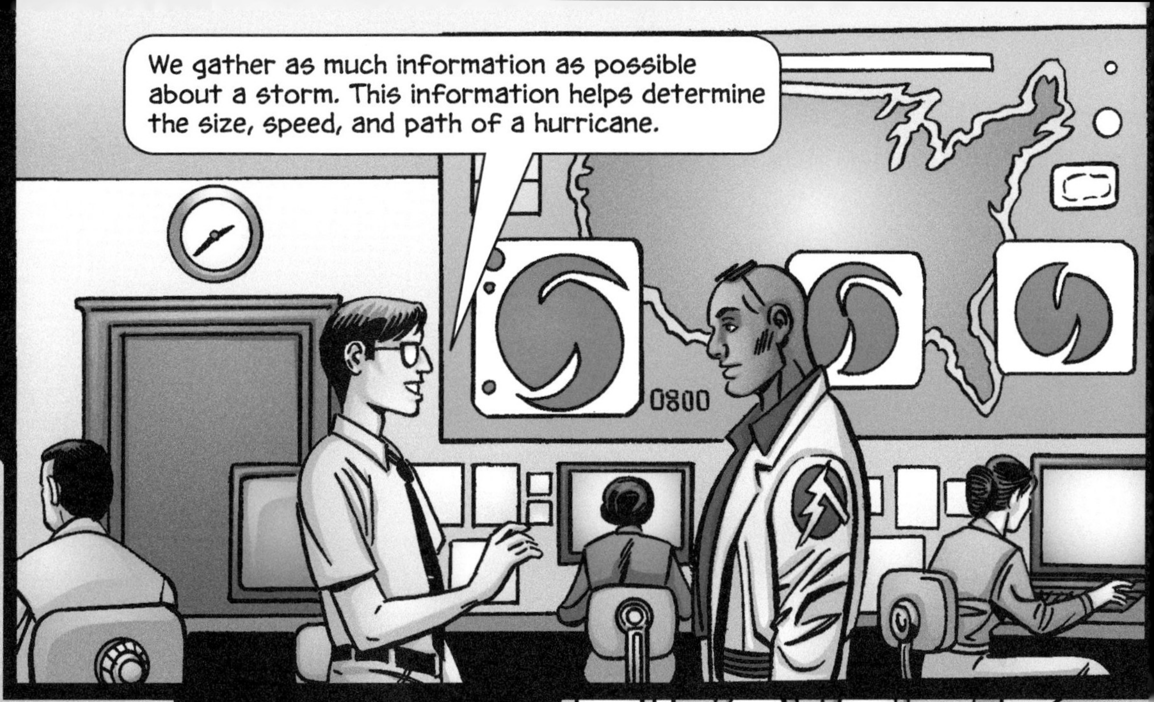
We gather as much information as possible about a storm. This information helps determine the size, speed, and path of a hurricane.
0800

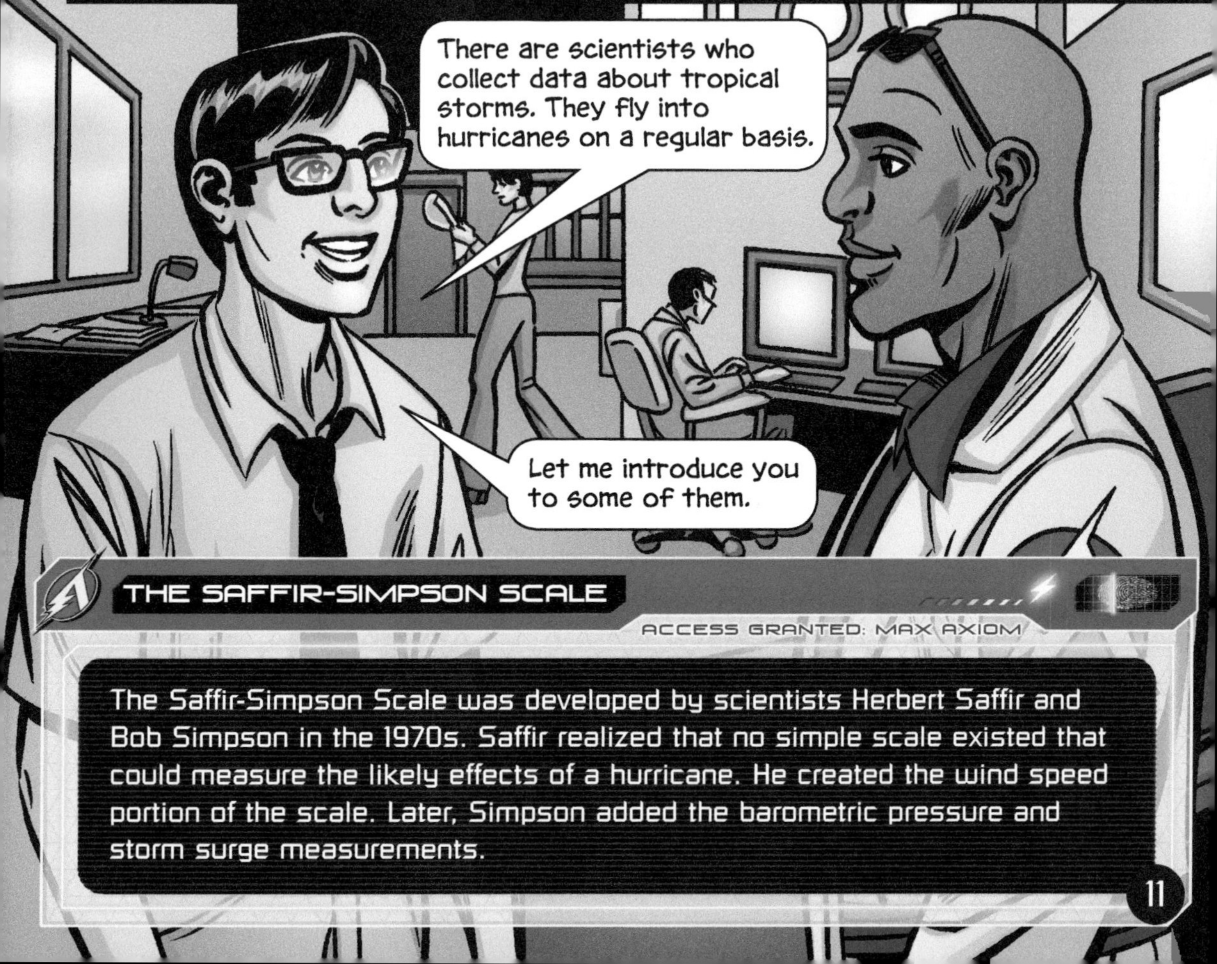
There are scientists who collect data about tropical storms. They fly into hurricanes on a regular basis.
Let me introduce you to some of them.

THE SAFFIR-SIMPSON SCALE

ACCESS GRANTED: MAX AXIOM

The Saffir-Simpson Scale was developed by scientists Herbert Saffir and Bob Simpson in the 1970s. Saffir realized that no simple scale existed that could measure the likely effects of a hurricane. He created the wind speed portion of the scale. Later, Simpson added the barometric pressure and storm surge measurements.

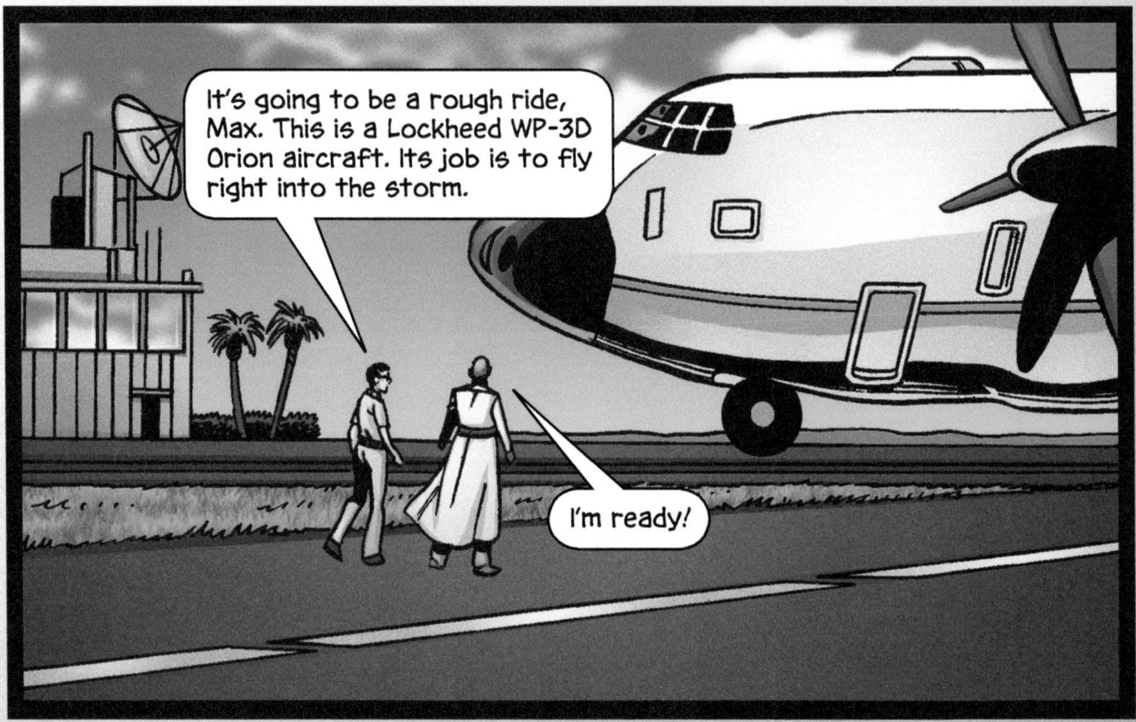
It's going to be a rough ride, Max. This is a Lockheed WP-3D Orion aircraft. Its job is to fly right into the storm.
I'm ready!

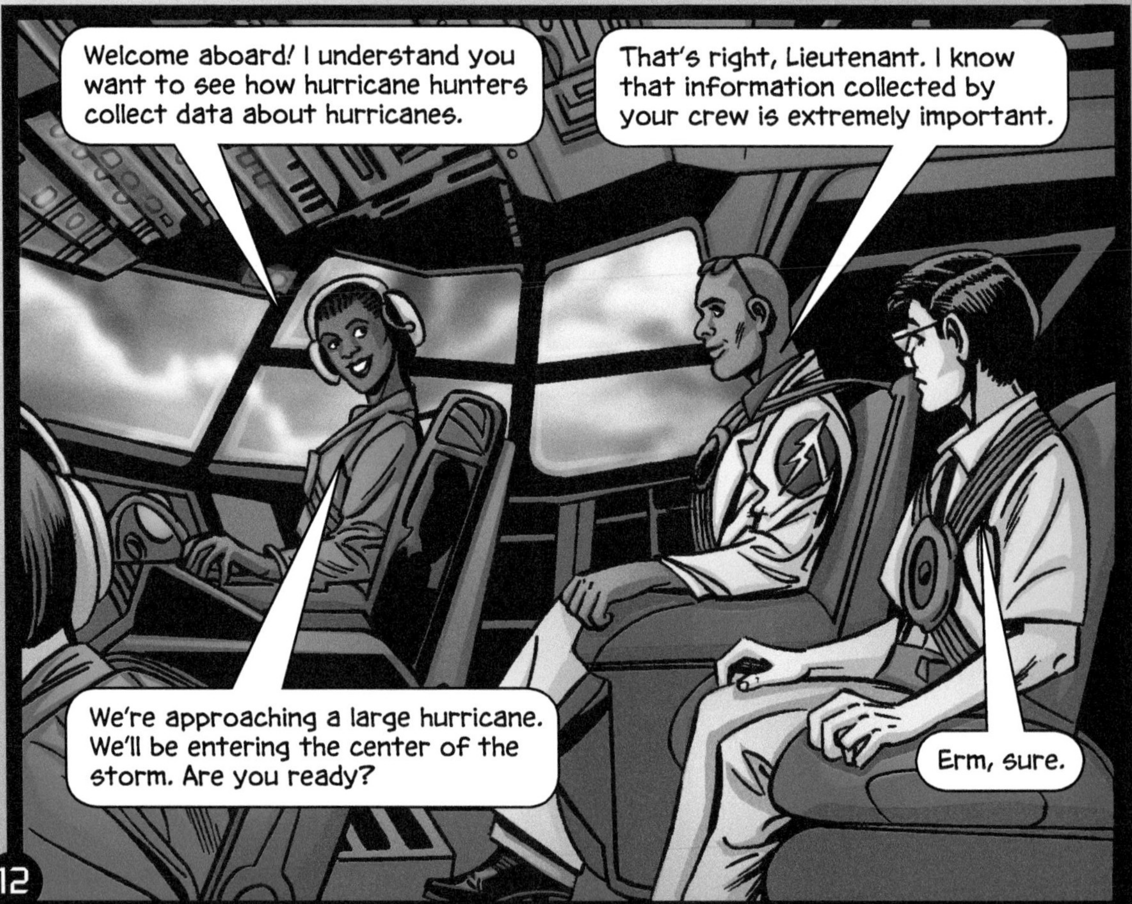
Welcome aboard! I understand you want to see how hurricane hunters collect data about hurricanes.
That's right, Lieutenant. I know that information collected by your crew is extremely important.
We're approaching a large hurricane. We'll be entering the center of the storm. Are you ready?
Erm, sure.

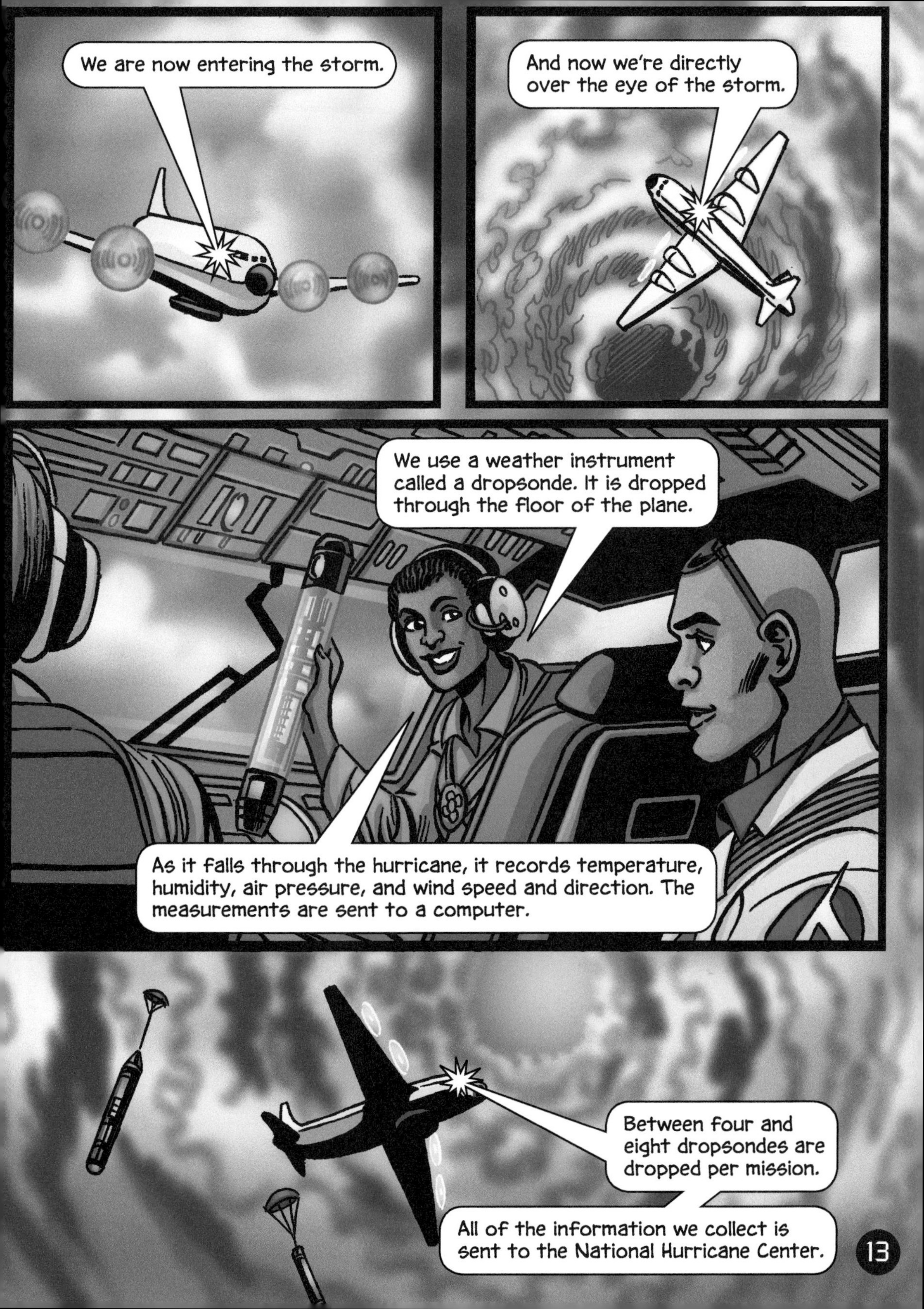

We are now entering the storm.
And now we're directly over the eye of the storm.
We use a weather instrument called a dropsonde. It is dropped through the floor of the plane.
As it falls through the hurricane, it records temperature, humidity, air pressure, and wind speed and direction. The measurements are sent to a computer.
Between four and eight dropsondes are dropped per mission.
All of the information we collect is sent to the National Hurricane Center.

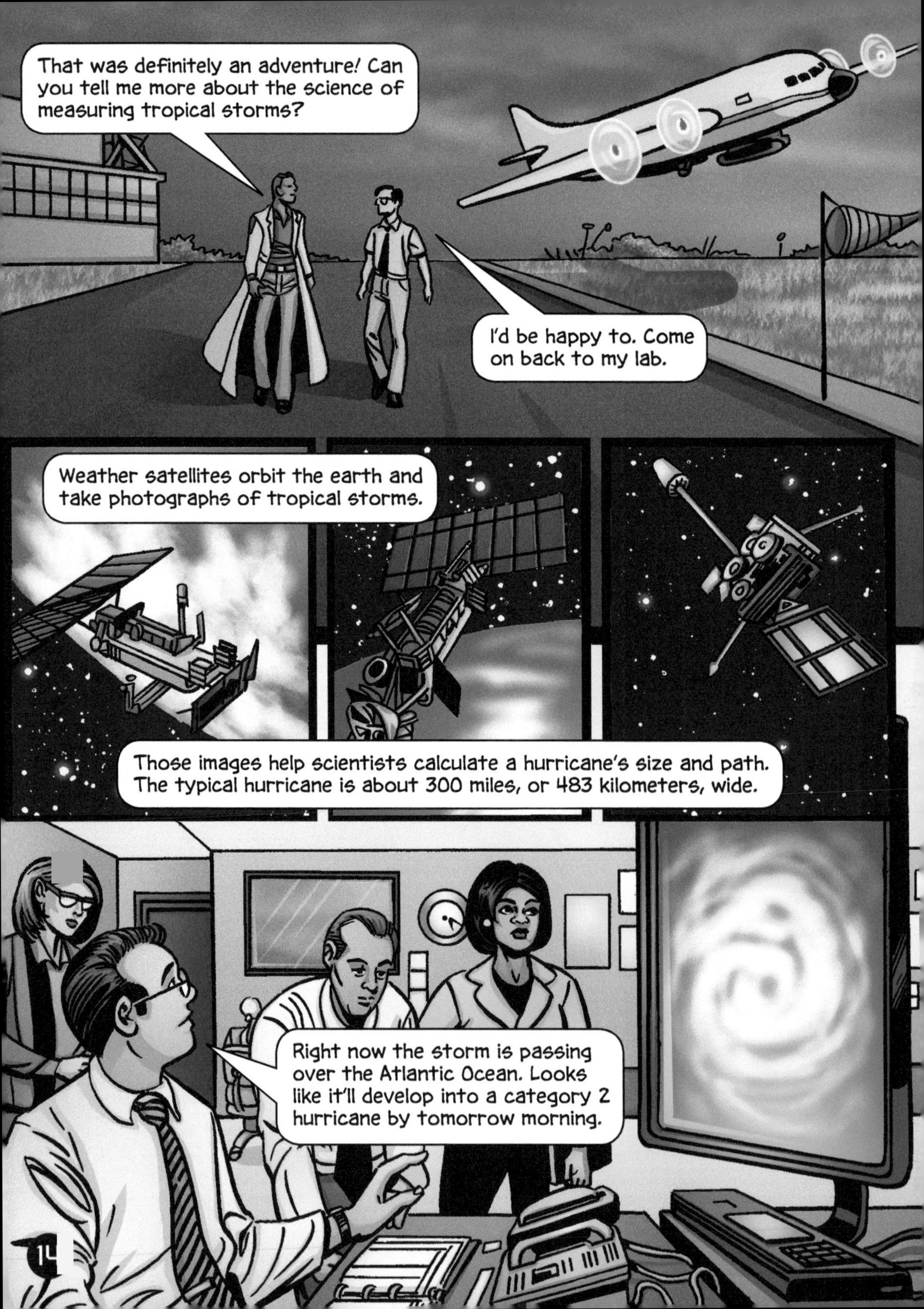
That was definitely an adventure! Can you tell me more about the science of measuring tropical storms?
I'd be happy to. Come on back to my lab.
Weather satellites orbit the earth and take photographs of tropical storms.
Those images help scientists calculate a hurricane's size and path. The typical hurricane is about 300 miles, or 483 kilometers, wide.
Right now the storm is passing over the Atlantic Ocean. Looks like it'll develop into a category 2 hurricane by tomorrow morning.

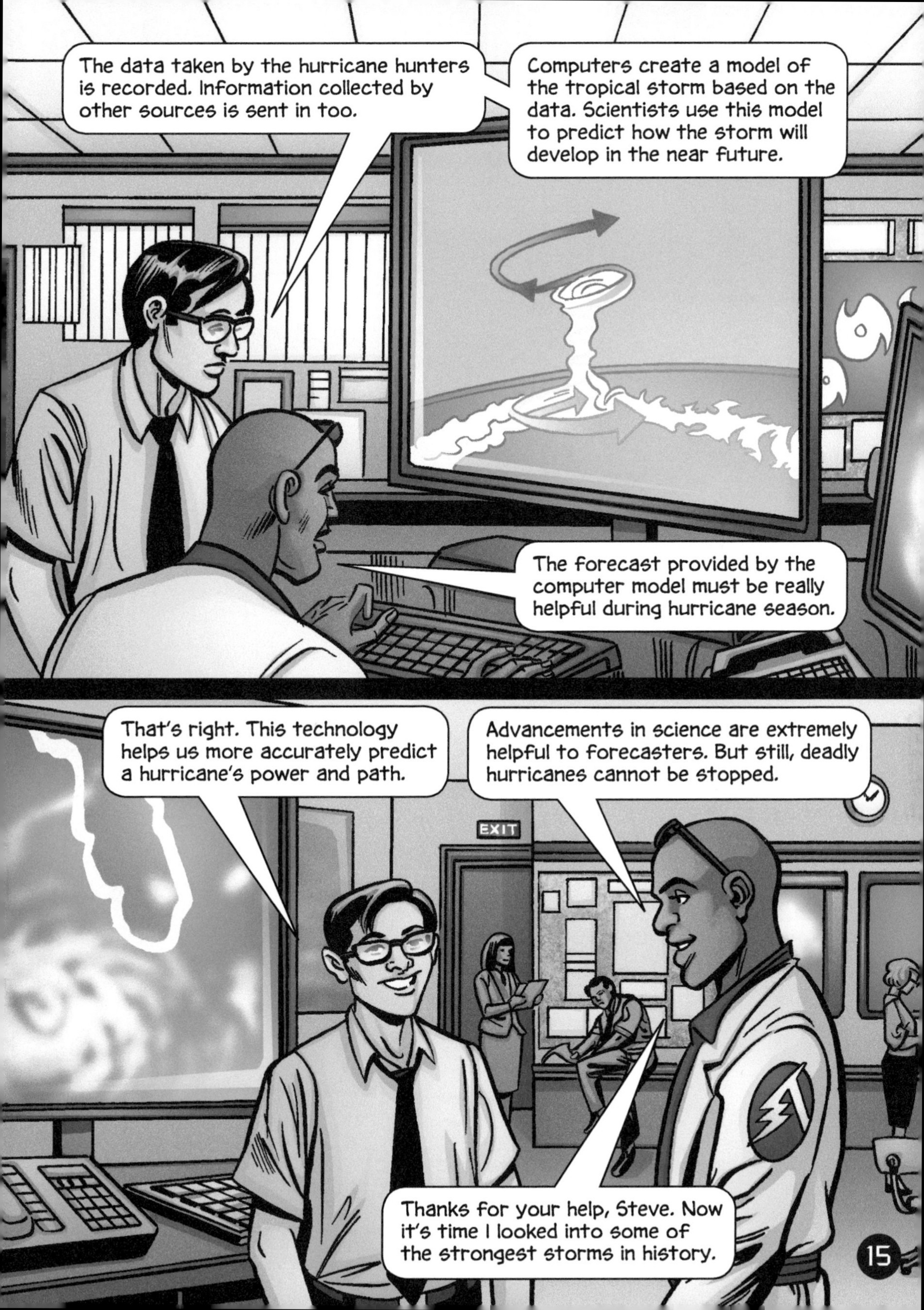

The data taken by the hurricane hunters is recorded. Information collected by other sources is sent in too.
Computers create a model of the tropical storm based on the data. Scientists use this model to predict how the storm will develop in the near future.
The forecast provided by the computer model must be really helpful during hurricane season.
That's right. This technology helps us more accurately predict a hurricane's power and path.
Advancements in science are extremely helpful to forecasters. But still, deadly hurricanes cannot be stopped.
EXIT
Thanks for your help, Steve. Now it's time I looked into some of the strongest storms in history.

SECTION 3

HURRICANES IN HISTORY

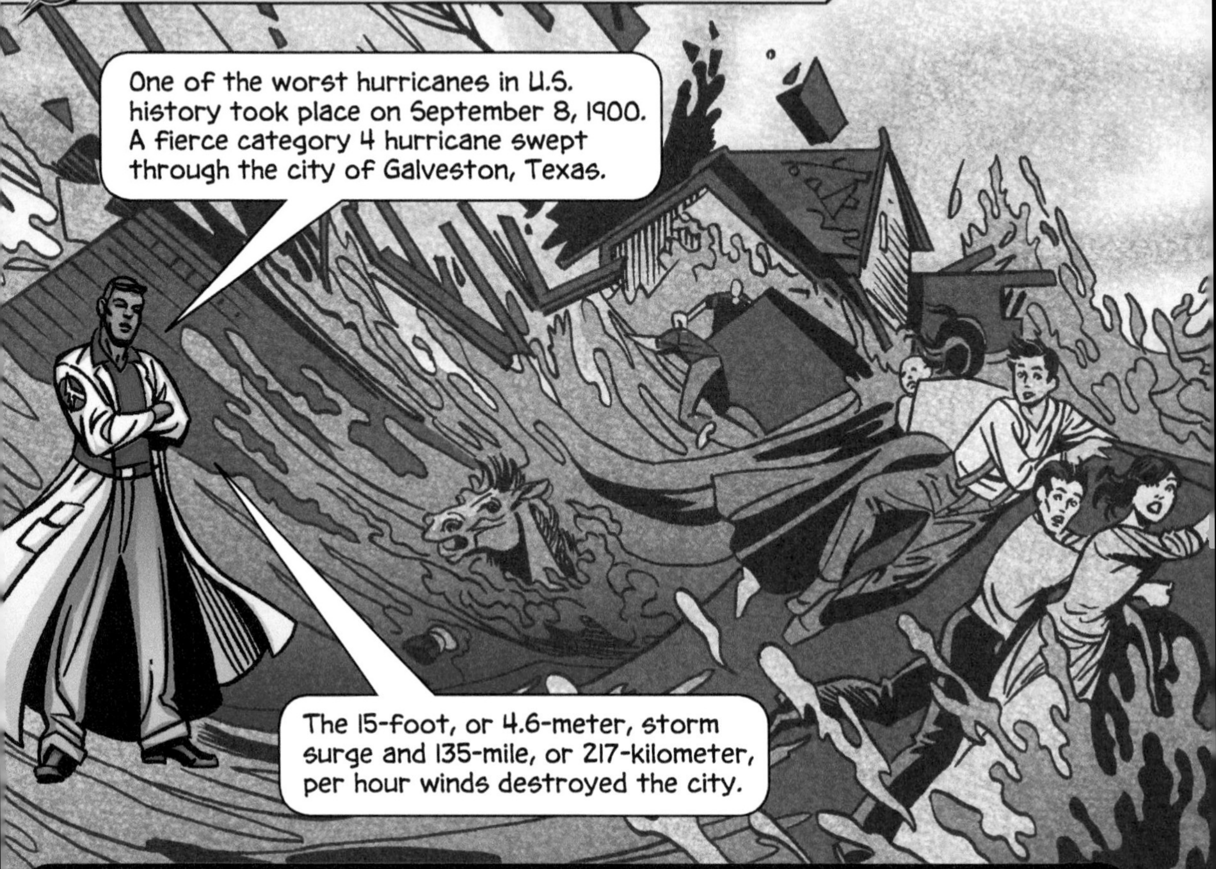
One of the worst hurricanes in U.S. history took place on September 8, 1900. A fierce category 4 hurricane swept through the city of Galveston, Texas.
The 15-foot, or 4.6-meter, storm surge and 135-mile, or 217-kilometer, per hour winds destroyed the city.

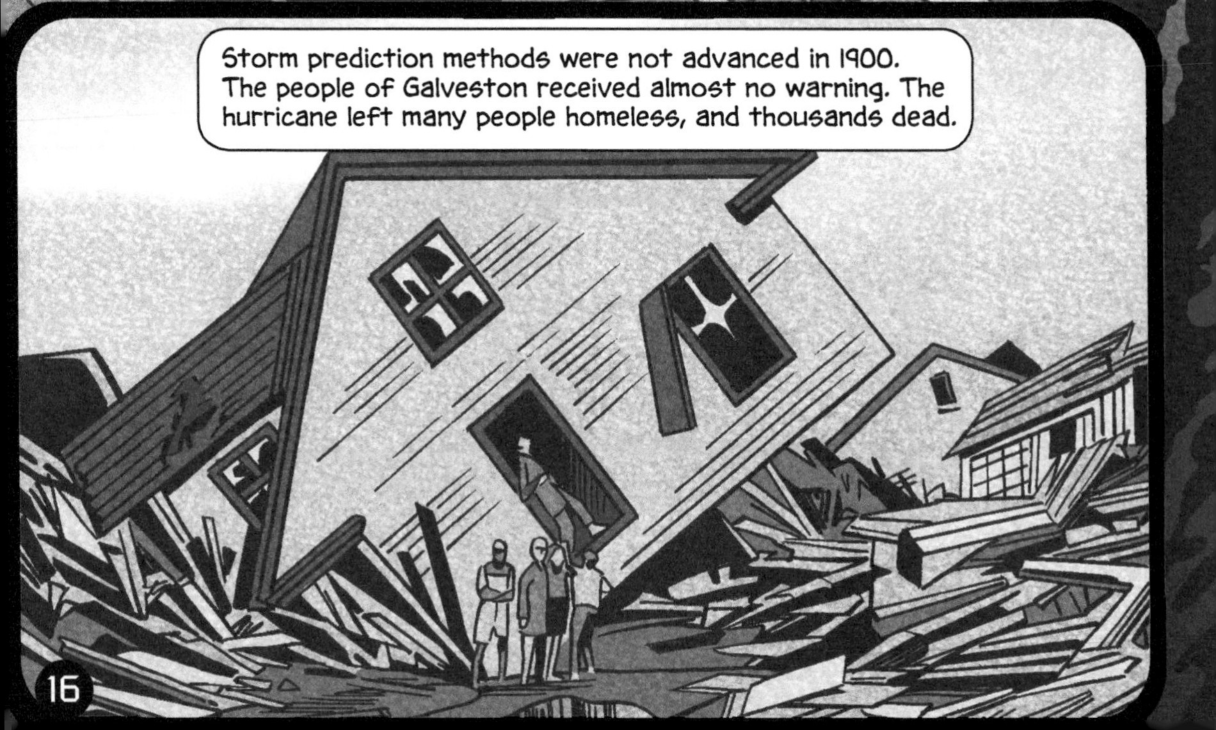
Storm prediction methods were not advanced in 1900. The people of Galveston received almost no warning. The hurricane left many people homeless, and thousands dead.

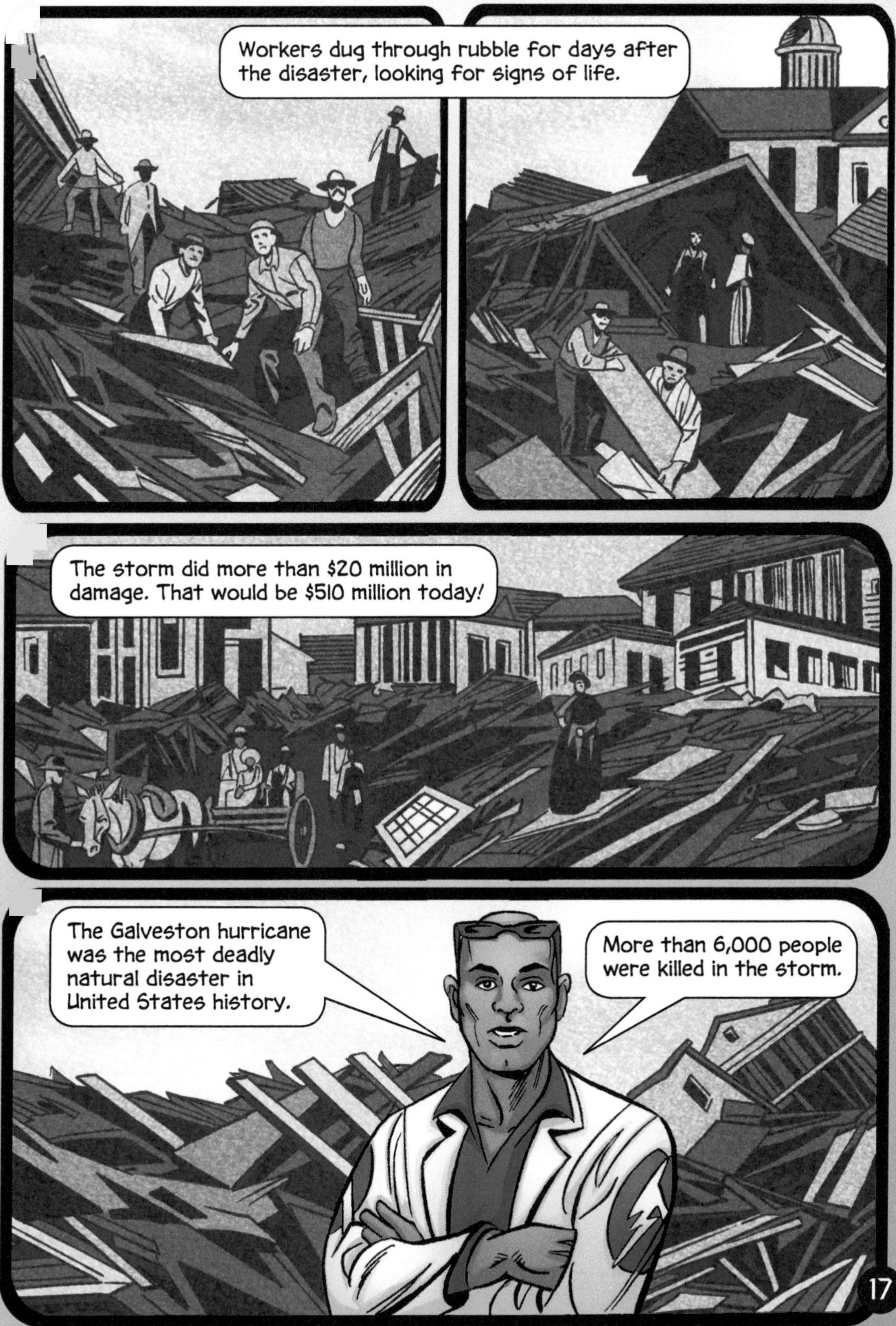

Workers dug through rubble for days after the disaster, looking for signs of life.
The storm did more than $20 million in damage. That would be $510 million today!
The Galveston hurricane was the most deadly natural disaster in United States history.
More than 6,000 people were killed in the storm.

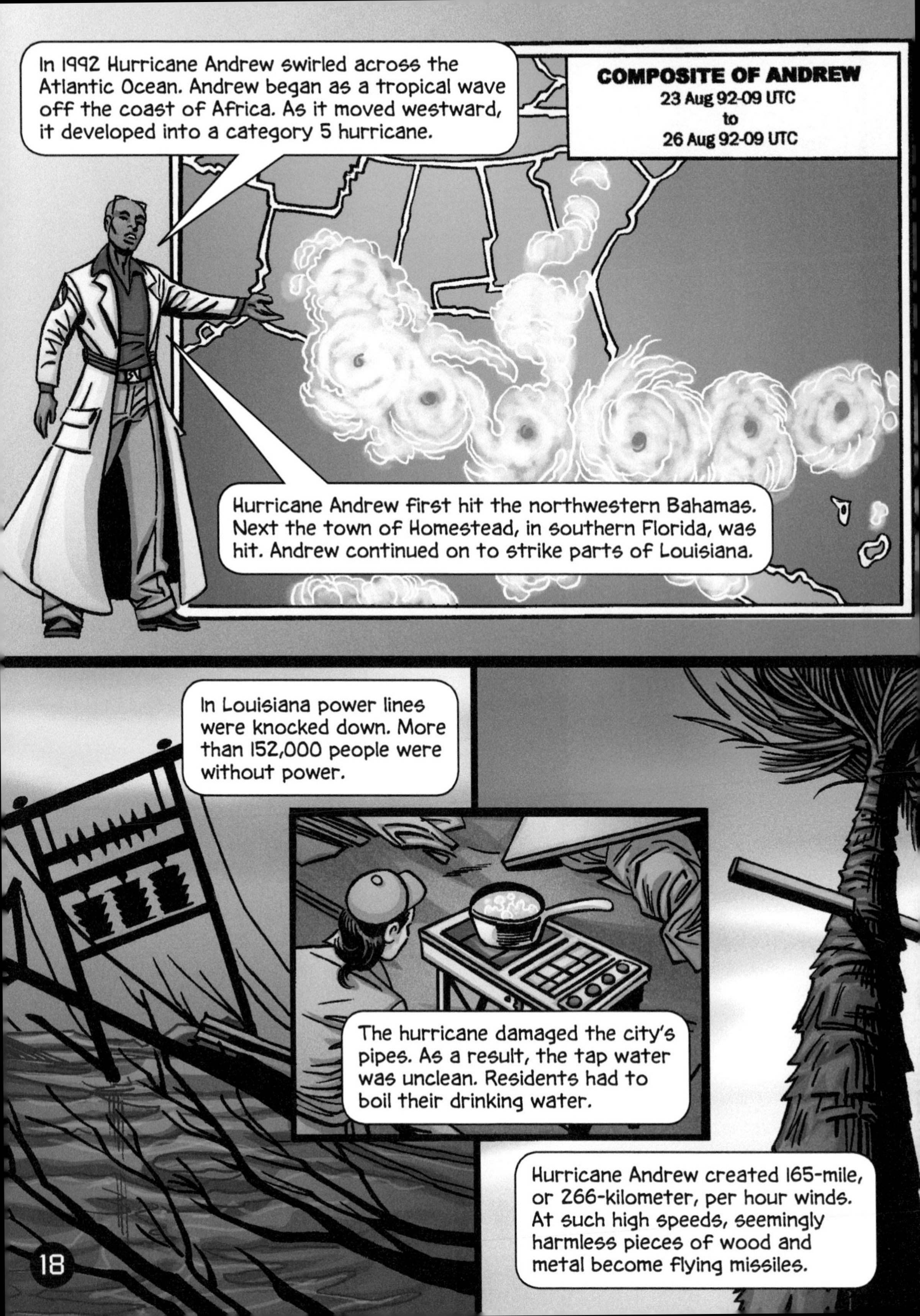
In 1992 Hurricane Andrew swirled across the Atlantic Ocean. Andrew began as a tropical wave off the coast of Africa. As it moved westward, it developed into a category 5 hurricane.
COMPOSITE OF ANDREW
23 Aug 92-09 UTC
to
26 Aug 92-09 UTC
Hurricane Andrew first hit the northwestern Bahamas. Next the town of Homestead, in southern Florida, was hit. Andrew continued on to strike parts of Louisiana.
In Louisiana power lines were knocked down. More than 152,000 people were without power.
The hurricane damaged the city's pipes. As a result, the tap water was unclean. Residents had to boil their drinking water.
Hurricane Andrew created 165-mile, or 266-kilometer, per hour winds. At such high speeds, seemingly harmless pieces of wood and metal become flying missiles.

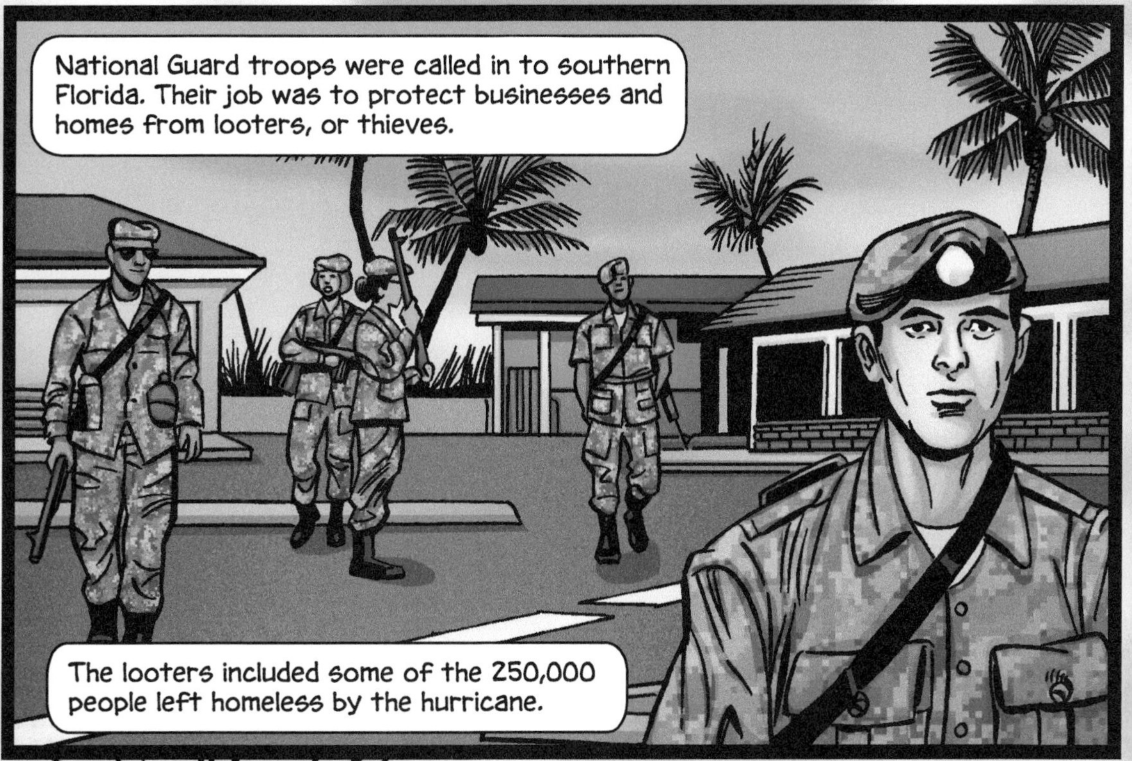
National Guard troops were called in to southern Florida. Their job was to protect businesses and homes from looters, or thieves.
The looters included some of the 250,000 people left homeless by the hurricane.

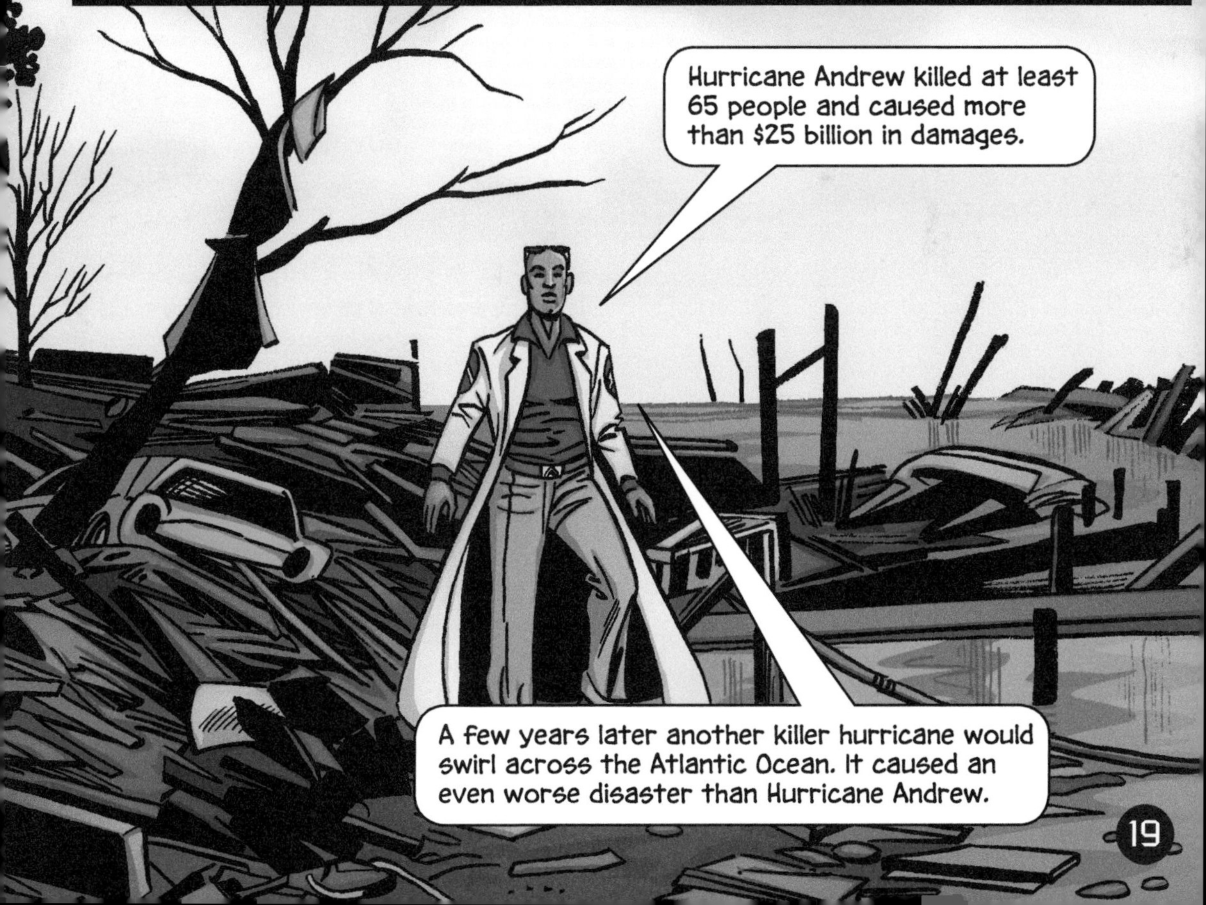
Hurricane Andrew killed at least 65 people and caused more than $25 billion in damages.
A few years later another killer hurricane would swirl across the Atlantic Ocean. It caused an even worse disaster than Hurricane Andrew.

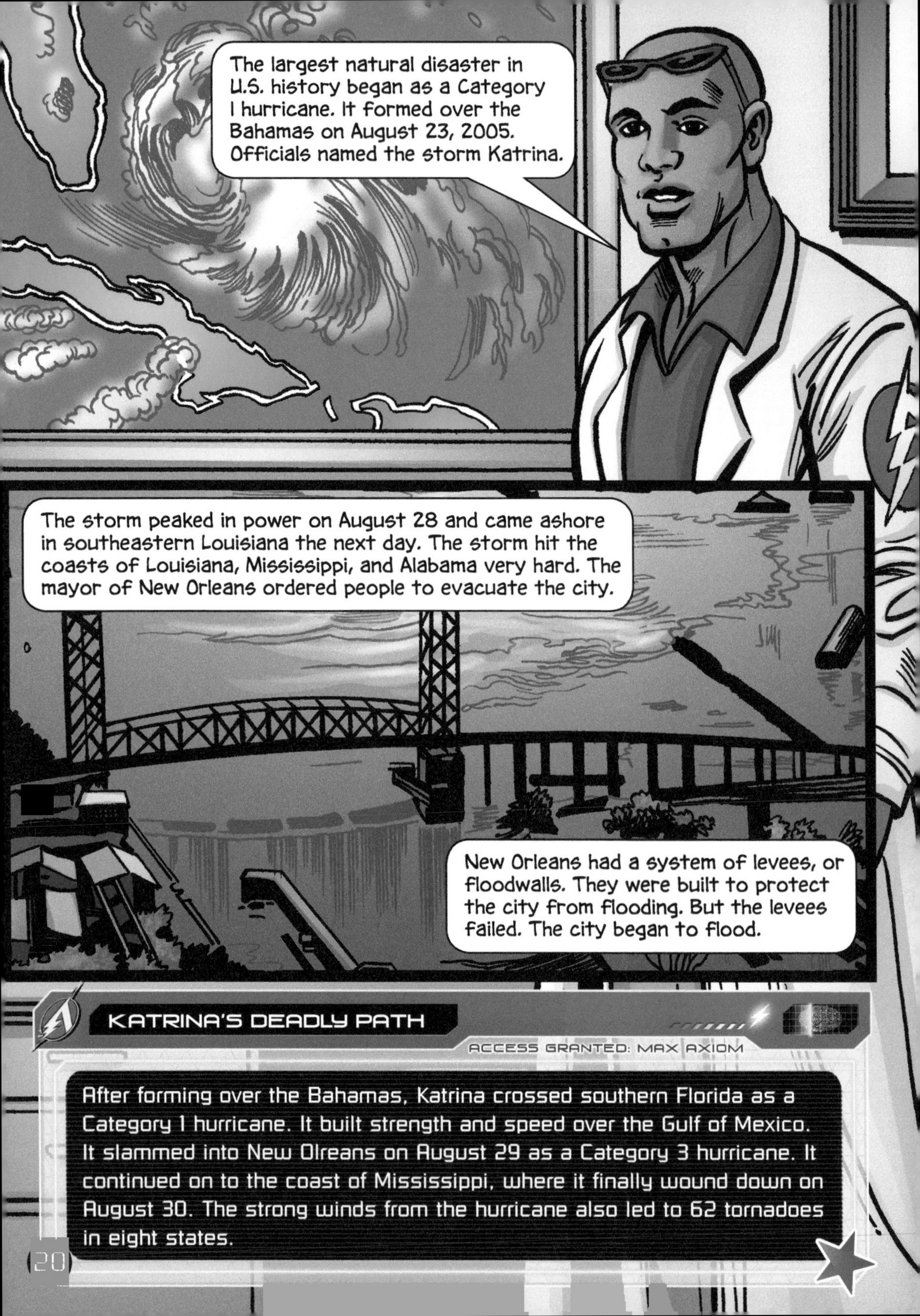
The largest natural disaster in U.S. history began as a Category 1 hurricane. It formed over the Bahamas on August 23, 2005. Officials named the storm Katrina.
The storm peaked in power on August 28 and came ashore in southeastern Louisiana the next day. The storm hit the coasts of Louisiana, Mississippi, and Alabama very hard. The mayor of New Orleans ordered people to evacuate the city.
New Orleans had a system of levees, or floodwalls. They were built to protect the city from flooding. But the levees failed. The city began to flood.

KATRINA'S DEADLY PATH

ACCESS GRANTED: MAX AXIOM

After forming over the Bahamas, Katrina crossed southern Florida as a Category 1 hurricane. It built strength and speed over the Gulf of Mexico. It slammed into New Olreans on August 29 as a Category 3 hurricane. It continued on to the coast of Mississippi, where it finally wound down on August 30. The strong winds from the hurricane also led to 62 tornadoes in eight states.

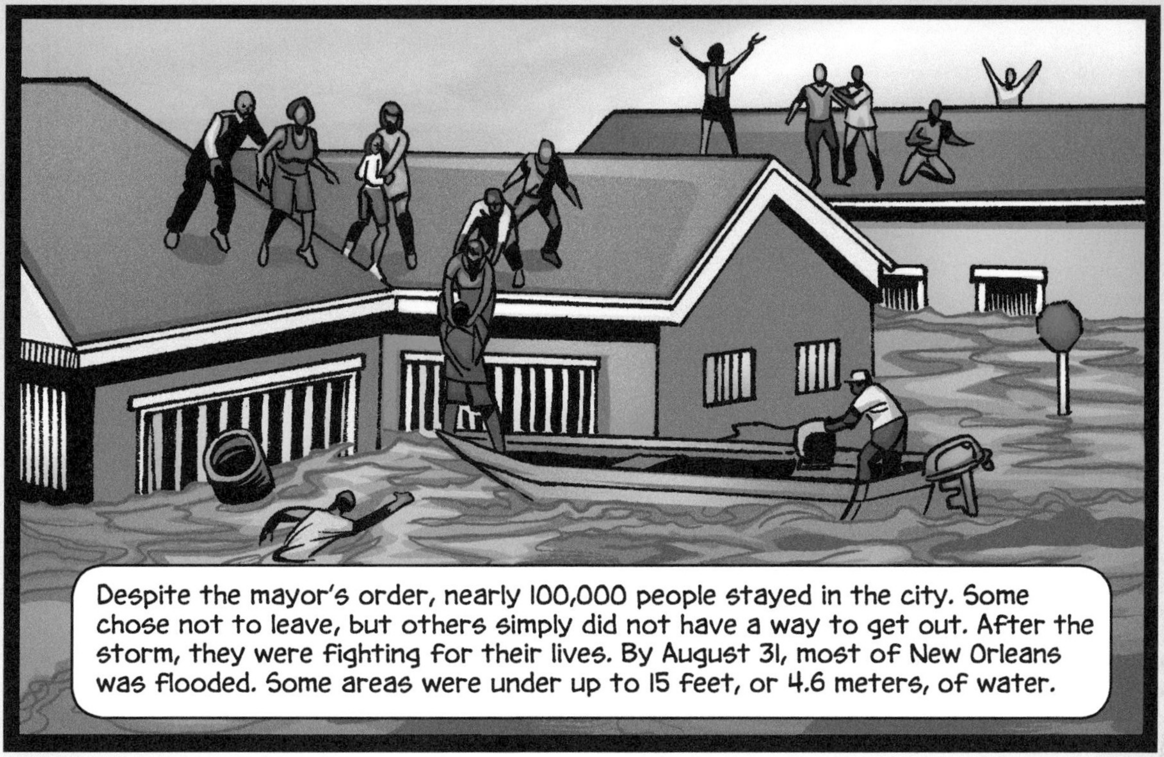
Despite the mayor's order, nearly 100,000 people stayed in the city. Some chose not to leave, but others simply did not have a way to get out. After the storm, they were fighting for their lives. By August 31, most of New Orleans was flooded. Some areas were under up to 15 feet, or 4.6 meters, of water.

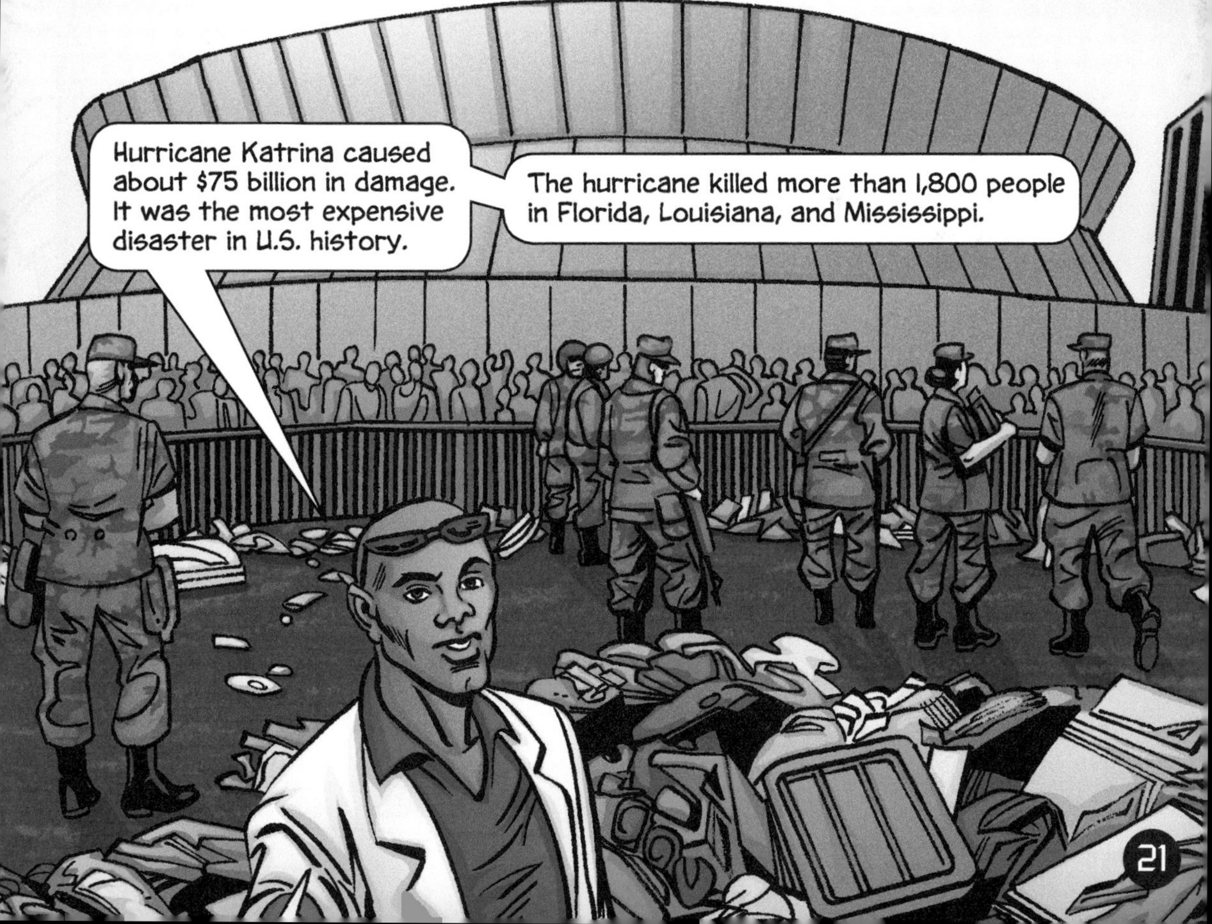
Hurricane Katrina caused about $75 billion in damage. It was the most expensive disaster in U.S. history.
The hurricane killed more than 1,800 people in Florida, Louisiana, and Mississippi.

SECTION 4 NAMING THE STORM

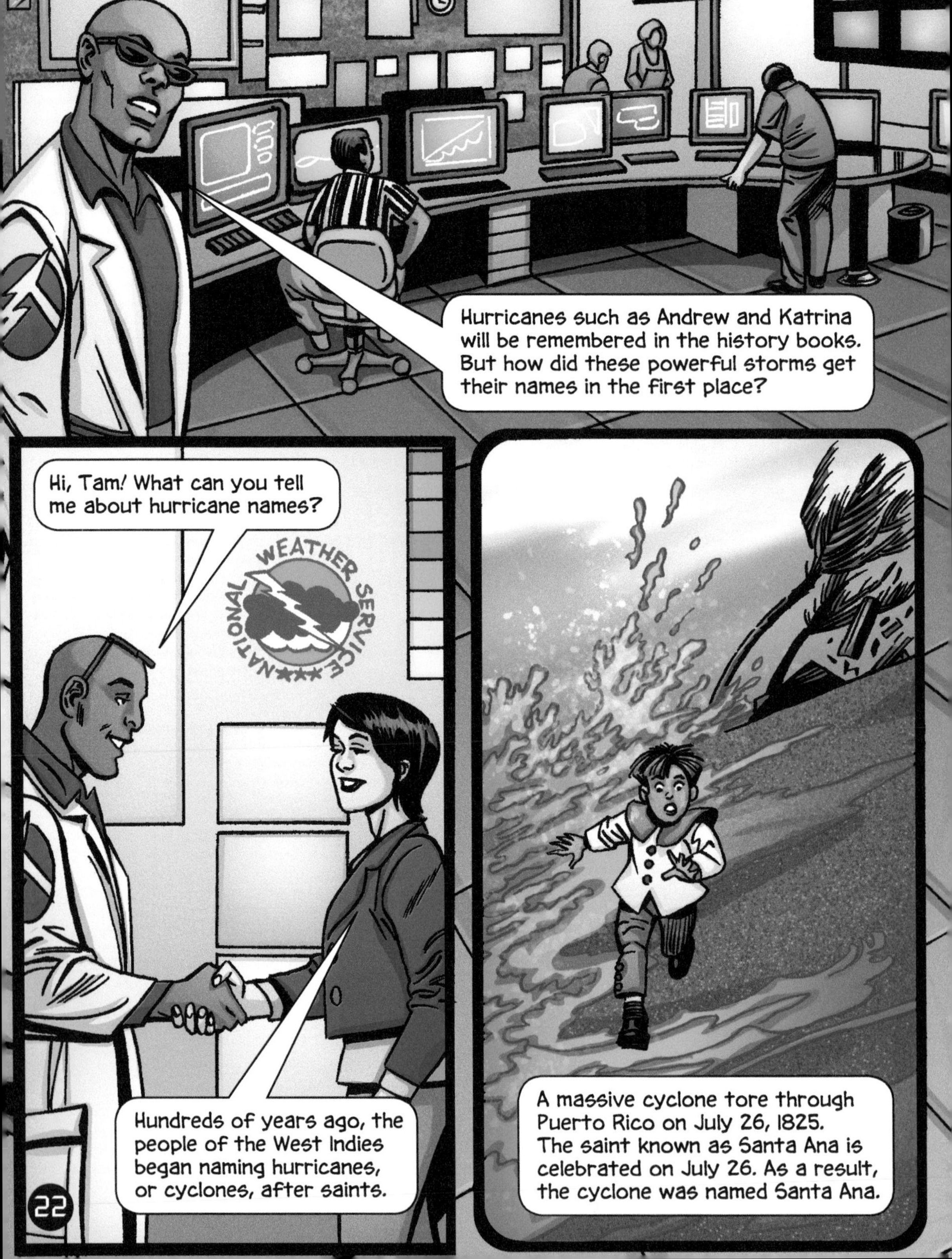
Hurricanes such as Andrew and Katrina will be remembered in the history books. But how did these powerful storms get their names in the first place?
Hi, Tam! What can you tell me about hurricane names?
NATIONAL WEATHER SERVICE
Hundreds of years ago, the people of the West Indies began naming hurricanes, or cyclones, after saints.
A massive cyclone tore through Puerto Rico on July 26, 1825. The saint known as Santa Ana is celebrated on July 26. As a result, the cyclone was named Santa Ana.

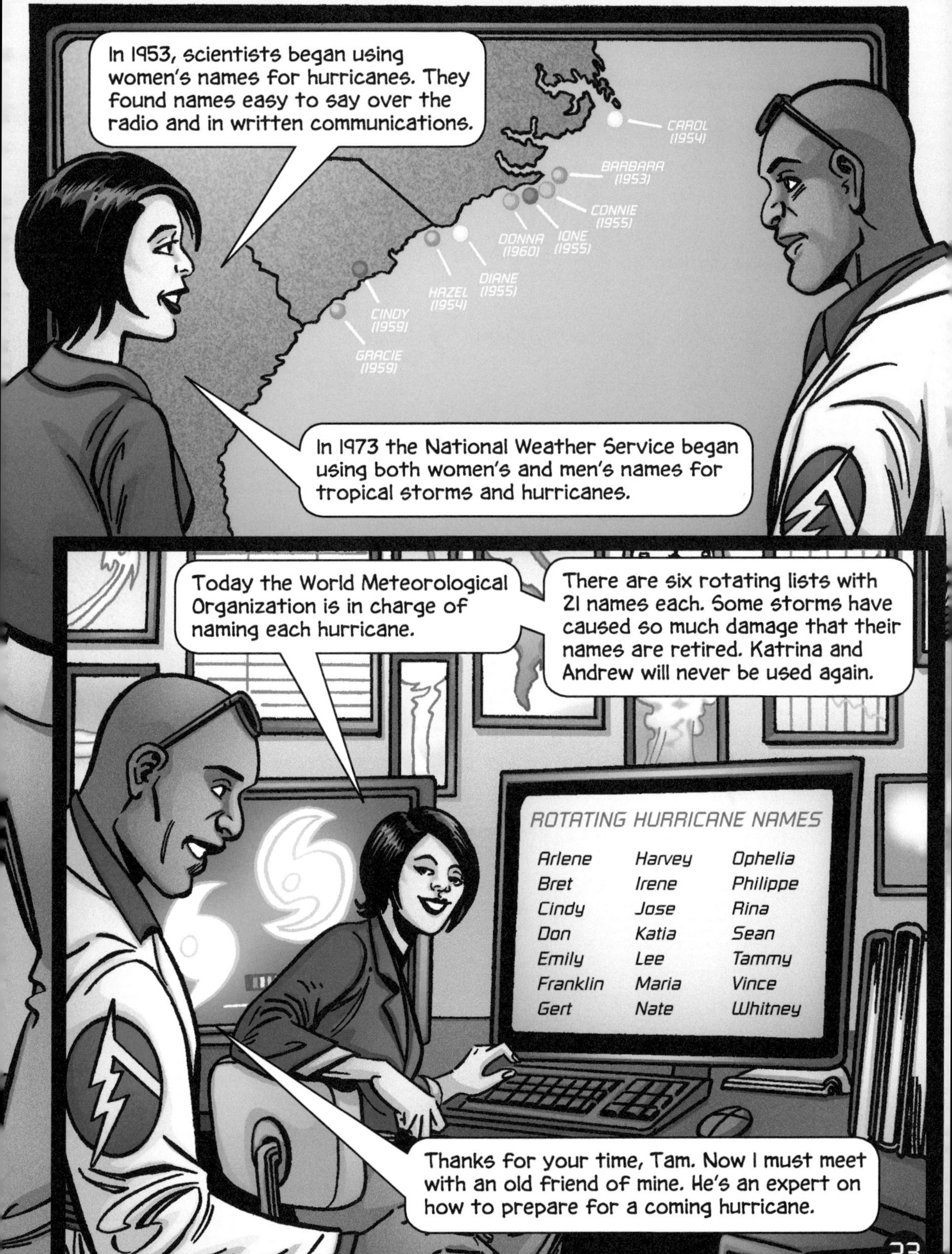
In 1953, scientists began using women's names for hurricanes. They found names easy to say over the radio and in written communications.
CAROL (1954)
BARBARA (1953)
CONNIE (1955)
DONNA (1960)
IONE (1955)
DIANE (1955)
HAZEL (1954)
CINDY (1959)
GRACIE (1959)
In 1973 the National Weather Service began using both women's and men's names for tropical storms and hurricanes.
Today the World Meteorological Organization is in charge of naming each hurricane.
There are six rotating lists with 21 names each. Some storms have caused so much damage that their names are retired. Katrina and Andrew will never be used again.
ROTATING HURRICANE NAMES
Arlene Harvey Ophelia
Bret Irene Philippe
Cindy Jose Rina
Don Katia Sean
Emily Lee Tammy
Franklin Maria Vince
Gert Nate Whitney
Thanks for your time, Tam. Now I must meet with an old friend of mine. He's an expert on how to prepare for a coming hurricane.

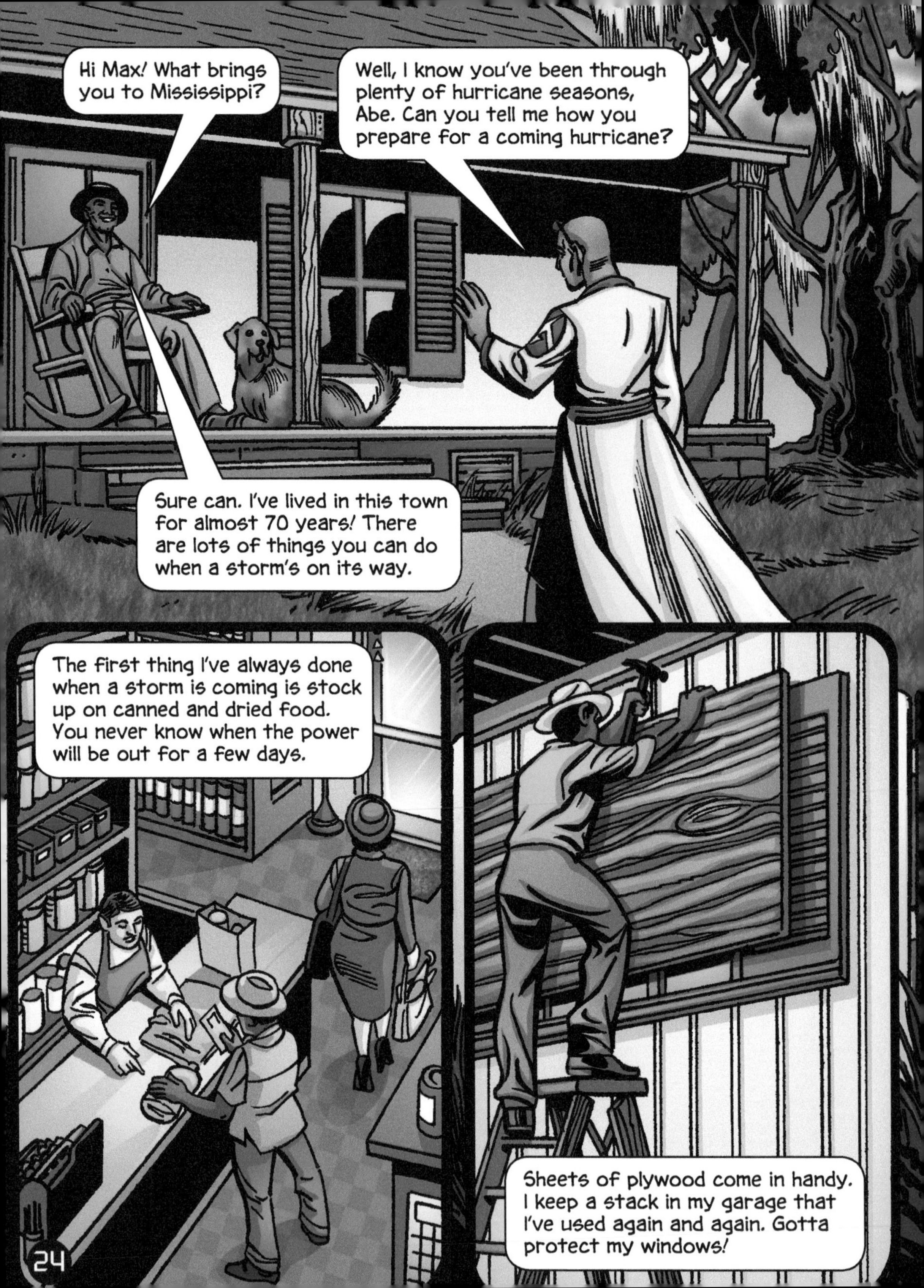

Hi Max! What brings you to Mississippi?
Well, I know you've been through plenty of hurricane seasons, Abe. Can you tell me how you prepare for a coming hurricane?
Sure can. I've lived in this town for almost 70 years! There are lots of things you can do when a storm's on its way.
The first thing I've always done when a storm is coming is stock up on canned and dried food. You never know when the power will be out for a few days.
Sheets of plywood come in handy. I keep a stack in my garage that I've used again and again. Gotta protect my windows!

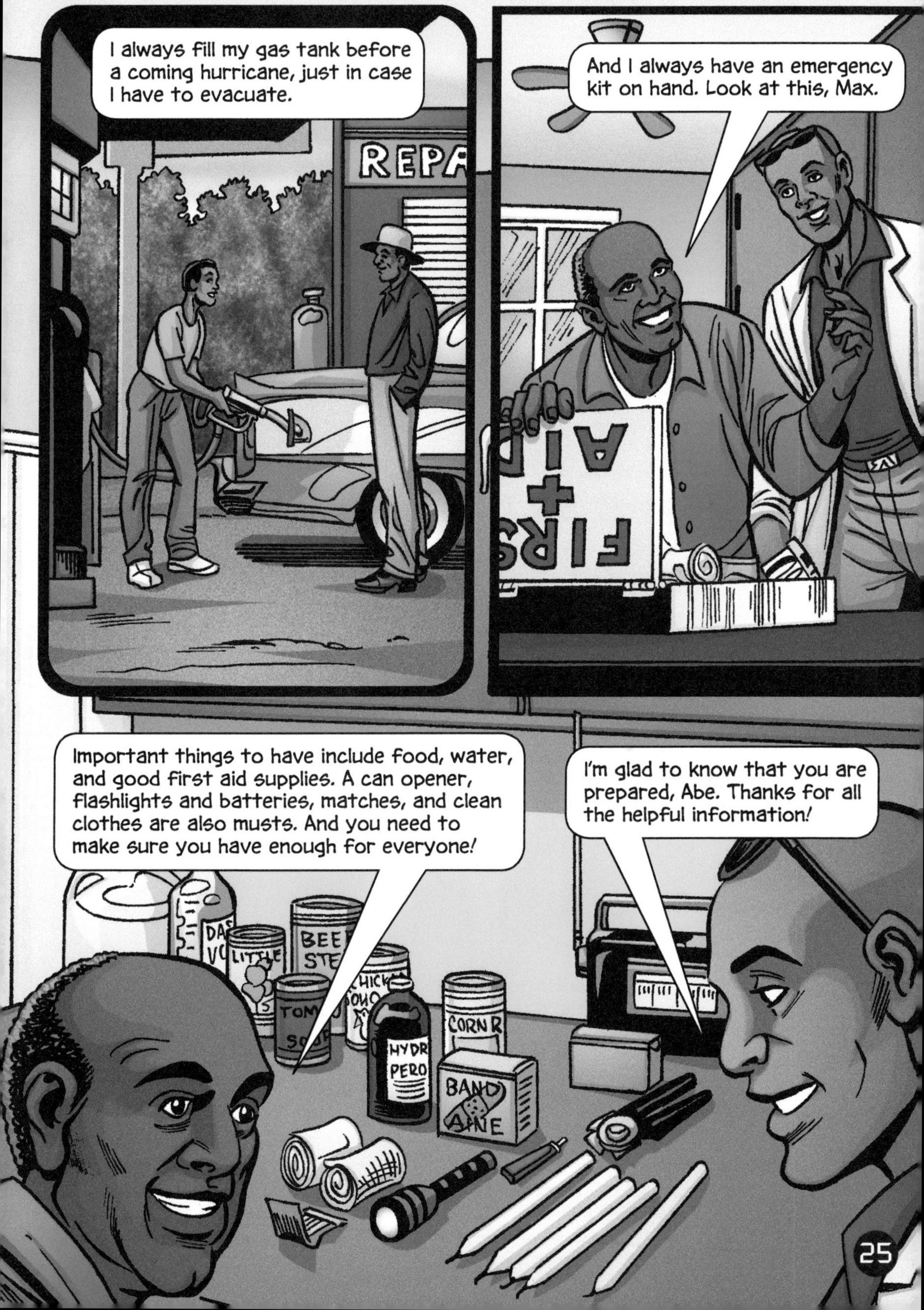
I always fill my gas tank before a coming hurricane, just in case I have to evacuate.
And I always have an emergency kit on hand. Look at this, Max.
Important things to have include food, water, and good first aid supplies. A can opener, flashlights and batteries, matches, and clean clothes are also musts. And you need to make sure you have enough for everyone!
I'm glad to know that you are prepared, Abe. Thanks for all the helpful information!

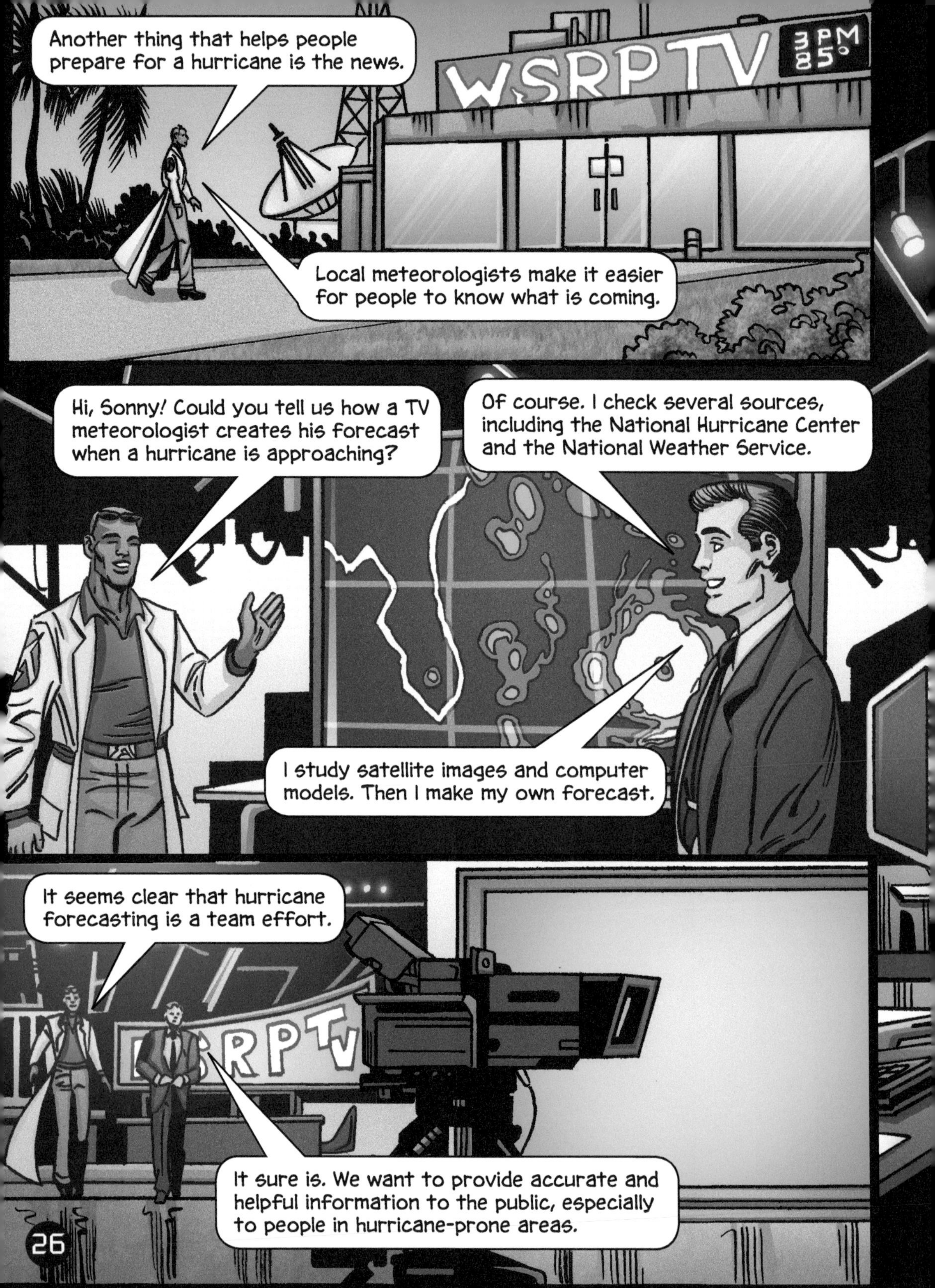
Another thing that helps people prepare for a hurricane is the news.
WSRP TV
3 PM 85°
Local meteorologists make it easier for people to know what is coming.
Hi, Sonny! Could you tell us how a TV meteorologist creates his forecast when a hurricane is approaching?
Of course. I check several sources, including the National Hurricane Center and the National Weather Service.
I study satellite images and computer models. Then I make my own forecast.
It seems clear that hurricane forecasting is a team effort.
It sure is. We want to provide accurate and helpful information to the public, especially to people in hurricane-prone areas.

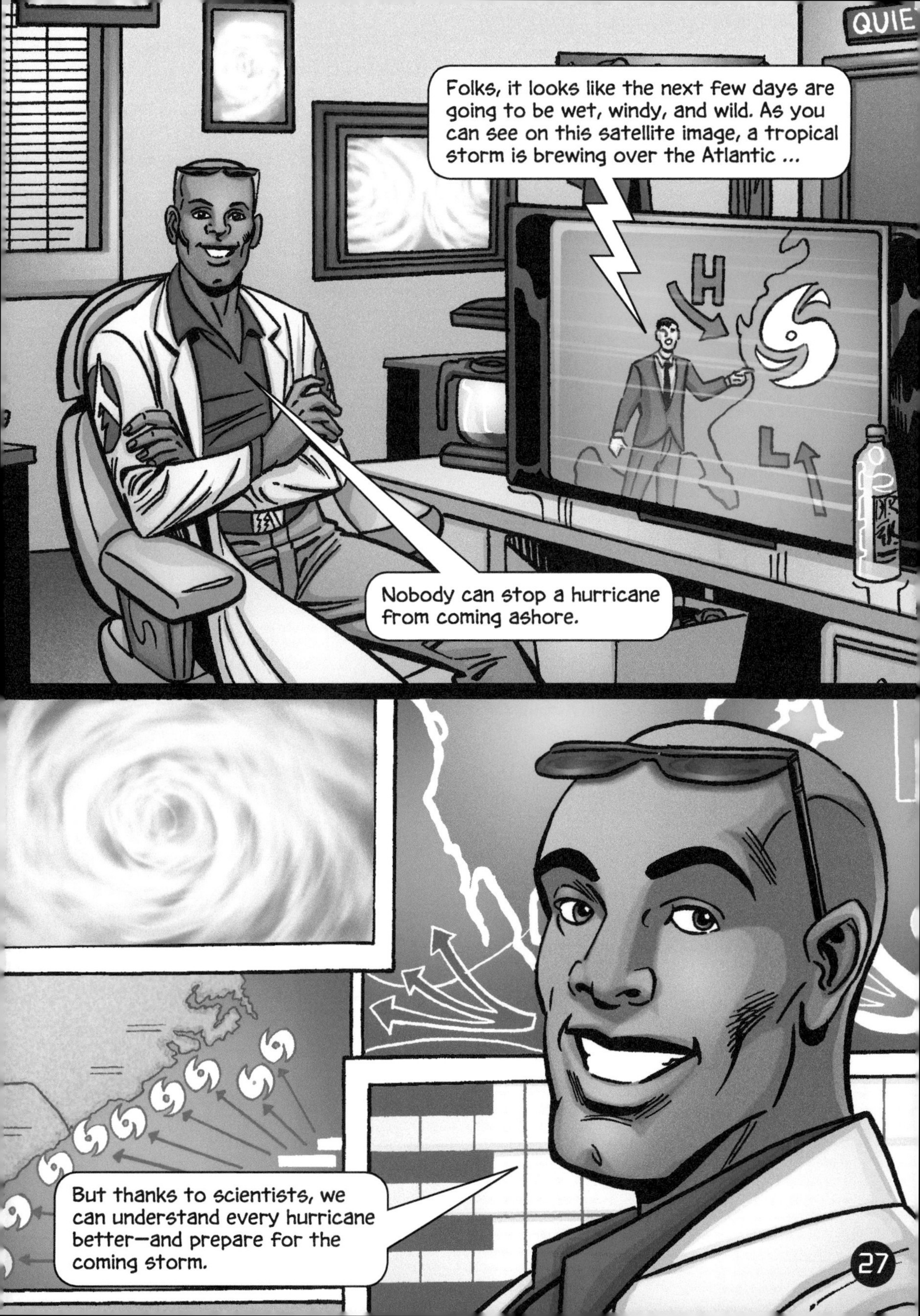
Folks, it looks like the next few days are going to be wet, windy, and wild. As you can see on this satellite image, a tropical storm is brewing over the Atlantic ...
Nobody can stop a hurricane from coming ashore.
But thanks to scientists, we can understand every hurricane better—and prepare for the coming storm.

HURRICANES

In order for a hurricane to form, ocean water must be at least 80 degrees Fahrenheit (27 degrees Celsius) down to a depth of 150 feet (46 meters). Many hurricanes that form simply spin out and fall apart over the ocean. Two or three hit the mainland of North America each year.

The official hurricane season over the Atlantic Ocean runs from June through November. The Pacific Ocean season is from mid-May through November.

In past years, scientists experimented with dropping chemicals into tropical storms to break the storms apart. This is no longer attempted because of a lack of funding and the ethical questions it creates.

A tropical storm's size has nothing to do with its strength. Sometimes a small storm can be very destructive and dangerous.

According to the National Hurricane Center, Florida has been hit with the most hurricanes.

All tropical storms spin counterclockwise in the Northern Hemisphere. They spin clockwise in the Southern Hemisphere.

The National Science Foundation did an investigation after Hurricane Katrina. They found design flaws in New Orleans' levees. They also found that the levees had not been maintained properly.

The U.S. military unofficially began using women's names to identify hurricanes during World War II. Soldiers named the storms after their wives or girlfriends.

Hurricanes are known as cyclones in the Bay of Bengal and northern Indian Ocean. The same type of weather system is called a typhoon in the western Pacific Ocean. Near Australia, it's known as a willy-willy.

MAKE A BAROMETER

Weather forecasters use barometers to measure atmospheric pressure and predict and track the strength of a hurricane. Make your own barometer to see how air pressure changes with the weather.

WHAT YOU NEED:

- scissors
- balloon
- glass jar
- rubber bands
- straw
- tape
- paper
- cardstock
- pencil

WHAT YOU DO:

1. Using the scissors, cut off the neck of the balloon. Make sure the opening will be large enough to fit over the top of the jar.

2. Wrap the balloon over the jar's opening until it stretches flat. Wrap rubber bands around the top of the jar to keep the balloon in place.

3. Tape one end of the straw to the center of the balloon.

4. Cut a tiny pointer out of cardstock. Insert the pointer into the end of the straw hanging off the jar.

5. Tape a sheet of paper to a wall. Place your jar near it so the pointer is close to the paper, but not actually touching it.

6. The pointer will rise and fall with changes in air pressure. Once a day, check the barometer and mark a line for each change you see. Take notes that describe what the weather is like when the pointer is higher and lower.

DISCUSSION QUESTIONS

1. Scientists have many ways to study hurricanes. How can scientists study hurricanes from the air?

2. Hurricanes generally begin in the same area and climate. Where do most hurricanes form and why?

3. What happens as a hurricane reaches the shore? Why are storm surges so dangerous?

4. What part of a hurricane is the calmest? Which part of the storm is the most violent? Explain why.

WRITING PROMPTS

1. Storm surges are huge domes of water created by hurricane winds. What are some of the effects of storm surges when they come ashore? Create a list of the effects.

2. Draw an aerial-view of a hurricane. Then write a brief description of how it formed and label its three main parts.

3. Hurricanes can be devastating to the areas they pass over. Imagine yourself as a reporter living through a hurricane. Write a news article describing the damage left behind.

4. Make a list of items you would include in a hurricane emergency kit for your family. Once your list is complete, organize the items from most important to least important.

GLOSSARY

barometric pressure (buh-RAH-meh-TRIK PRESH-ur)—changes in air pressure; barometric pressure is measured by a barometer

dropsonde (DROP-sahnd)—an information collecting device used to obtain information related to hurricanes and weather prediction

evacuate (i-VA-kyuh-wayt)—to leave an area during a time of danger

eye (EYE)—the central, calm area at the center of a hurricane

eye wall (EYE WAHL)—the tall, vertical wall of fast-moving clouds lining the outer edge of a hurricane's eye

levee (LEH-vee)—a long, continuous wall that protects a coastal area from flooding

meteorologist (mee-tee-ur-AWL-uh-jist)—a person who studies and predicts the weather

rain band (RAYN band)—a spiral arc of thunderstorms around tropical storms, especially hurricanes

Saffir-Simpson Scale (SAF-fir SIMP-suhn SKALE)—a scale from one to five that rates a hurricane based on its wind speed; the scale helps experts guess how much damage and flooding the hurricane might cause

storm surge (STORM SURJ)—a sudden, strong rush of water that happens as a hurricane moves onto land

tropical depression (TRAH-pu-kuhl di-PRE-shuhn)—ocean thunderstorm having winds of less than 39 mph (63 kph)

tropical storm (TRAH-pu-kuhl STORM)—ocean thunderstorm having winds from 39 to 73 mph (63 to 117 kph)

READ MORE

Abdo, Kenny. *How to Survive a Hurricane*. Abdo Edina, MN: Abdo Group, 2018.

Gagliardi, Sue. *Hurricane Katrina*. Mendota Heights, MN: North Star Editions, 2019.

Lew, Kristi. *Hurricanes*. Nature's Mysteries. New York, NY: The Rosen Publishing Group, Incorporated, 2019.

INTERNET SITES

National Geographic Kids: Hurricane
https://kids.nationalgeographic.com/explore/science/hurricane/#hurricane-aletta.jpg

Science Kids: Hurricane Facts for Kids
http://www.sciencekids.co.nz/sciencefacts/weather/hurricane.html

Weather Wiz Kids: Hurricanes
http://www.weatherwizkids.com/weather-hurricane.htm

Super-cool stuff! Check out projects, games, and lots more at **www.capstonekids.com**

INDEX